An Unimaginable Step

Tim Gidley

Published by Crown Voice Ministries Publishing

P.O. Box 1077
Mango, FL 33550

http://www.crownvoiceministries.com

TABLE OF CONTENTS

Introduction

It has been a Delight and Joy to write this book *An Unimaginable Step*. Reviewing how God has blessed our family and led us through this faith journey has inspired me and my family to keep everything on the altar of sacrifice and to do at anytime what our LORD commands. Evangelist Reinhard Bonnke insisted, "Stepping out into Faith isn't stepping into darkness, but stepping into the light."

You will see in this book that as we stepped out into our amazing season all that we required was brought forth by the hand of God joined BY FAITH! Our family became stronger and even more joyful as we went. We couldn't use our eyes, we had to use our faith and knowledge that God said is exactly what He would do.

We understood what Romans 4 meant when Paul said that Abraham was fully persuaded that God would do what He said He would do.

I have to say that my wife Sabrina was amazing during this 40,000 mile journey. She supported the vision from day one until June 24th of 2019 when we arrived back in South Carolina. She has always encouraged me and continues to desire a life that is fully engaged in only the will of God. Sabrina always quotes Pastor Adonica Howard-Browne, "God's Will. Nothing More, Nothing Less, and Nothing Else."

My children Maximus, Giselle, and Grace are the most precious, rare kids on the earth. Wherever and Whatever situation they find themselves, they are ready to pray and believe God right along with their mother and me. We would never hide any challenges we might experience so that when God provides they are able to rejoice with us. I am a firm believer that we must prepare our children to obey God and trust him. That way they are prepared for life and the adventure God has for them.

I desire to thank John Mason, my friend first and advisor secondly. John has been the head of three publishing companies and has sold millions of books. We were recently on the phone and I was asking John about suggestions for a title. John told me, "Tim, what you and your family did was AN UNIMAGINABLE STEP."

I said, "John, what did you just say?" I asked because the witness of the Holy Spirit overwhelmed my heart with a thrill of delight. It's God's way of confirming that what you heard or said is RIGHT and in line with His will. HIS CHOICE!!! He repeated himself. I said, "My brother, you just gave me the title to our book."

You will find in this book that God used many people to help us obey Him and accomplish his purpose. My family and I would like to express our heart-felt appreciation to the following people. Dave and Mandy (and Molly) Reed, Rick and Debbie McMeans, Randy and Ginger Bumgardner, Evan and Shawnna Perez and their kiddos Tatum and Hunter, Dr. Rick and Karen Boyle, Pastors Kevin and Jennifer Martin, Drs. Arlin and Kris Smith, Richard Page, Dr. Andy and Geri Kartsen, Pastors Leland and Cyntian Wesson, Gary and Terry Del Gorgio, Gus and Karen Bess and the Band of Brothers, Pastor Steve Calanga, Dr. Robert Derryberry, Addie Campbell and the Ladies of Coffee Talk, Pastors Pep and Angie Robey, Pastor Samuel Lee of Korean Covenant Church and our San Francisco Family, Pastor James Wright, Greg and Courtney Hand, Dr. Ron Halvorson, Mike and Nichol Pangkee, Sandy

Pangkee, Becky Pillow and the rest of Bethel
Christian School and Church in Riverside, CA.
Thank you Pastors Rodney and Adonica Howard-
Browne and finally, thanks to Drs. Drake and
Serena Travis for the remarkable editing job on
this book.

God has people and connection for you just
as He did us. The answer when it comes to Our
Father in Heaven is always YES!!! As the ole hymn
says, "Yes, Lord, Yes, to your will and to your way."

May you be blessed and encouraged. And
may you be disturbed if required, of course. My
favorite singer is Larnelle Harris and he sings a
song titled "Disturb Us Lord." I pray that if you
have delayed or you have put off what God is
speaking to your heart to do that you will repent,
refire, ignite and dive headlong into the will of
Almighty God. No more delay. Great things are
in store for you, your family, church, ministry
and Life. A mentor from long ago Dr. Loran
Helm always said. Walking with God is THRILLS,
ROMANCE AND ADVENTURE.

My family and I encourage you to obey God and
take AN UNIMAGINABLE STEP!!!

Romans 16:9a

For your obedience is come abroad unto all men.

CHAPTER 1

Grace, Go Turn On the Light

Well, here we go. Have you ever known that God had placed something in your heart to do, but the task was outside of what was known and comfortable? Sure you have, and that is where I begin this book.

I love to sing and I enjoy speaking to crowds of people regarding the faithfulness of my God to me and my family. But writing? It is different. But if I have learned anything, it is that God will require you to do something that is outside the norm so that you must put a "demand" on your faith. You must go toward what is impossible so that you can rely squarely on HIM. He simply wants you to depend on Him.

I love to tell the story of a time a few years ago when our youngest, Gabrielle Grace, was a 3 or 4 year old cutie. Sometimes we stick to calling her

Gabriella Grace but mostly we call her Grace and sometimes BOONIES (don't ask Laugh Out Loud [LOL]!). I looked at her and said, "Grace, go and turn the light on for Daddy."

Now the light switch was too high for her and it would be impossible for her to reach the light switch. But she didn't let that stop her from obeying her Daddy. I had made a request and she was going to do her best. Now I knew she wasn't able to reach the light and I knew she had no ability to do what I had asked. But her desire to please me and obey just thrilled my Daddy's Heart. She turned and walked across the room.

What she didn't see was that I was walking behind her. As she neared the light switch, I put my hands under her arms and lifted her up and she switched on the light. As I put her down, I said, "Thank you, Gracie."

She turned and looked at me and said, "YOU'RE WELCOME!!!" LOL!

Do you see where I'm going with this example? My heart was blessed as a Father that my girl just turned to obey my request. She didn't think, "That is too tough for me, what is my Dad thinking giving me such an impossible task?" She simply obeyed and I was there to lift her up. I can remember doing this and hearing the

Holy Spirit whisper to me, "You are acting as the GRACE OF GOD."

WOW!!! All I or you need to do is obey what He says to do and His ability, His power, His grace is there to do all the heavy lifting. You just hear and turn around and go in the direction that He says GO.

This simplistic story is really what helped me and my family consider taking an unimaginable step of faith and begin the most radical stage of obedience that we had ever experienced. Like I said....HERE WE GO!!!

MATTHEW 21:22

And all things, whatsoever ye shall ask in prayer, believing, ye shall receive.

CHAPTER 2

You're Outta Here in 60 Days

In October 2017, I felt a deep call from the Holy Spirit to commune with Him in a deeper way. I couldn't really put my finger on it, but I knew that God desired for me to wait upon Him in prayer, the Word, and observation. OBSERVATION?

My Prayer Journey as a Teenager

I had prayed before. As a kid, I was kinda weird I guess. I loved the Lord. I thought, "Who wouldn't desire to know the God of the Universe? Why wouldn't you like to commune and become close with the one who spoke LIGHT BE?" I began waiting upon the Lord when I was around 14 years old. Many times I had spent an hour or two just praying and talking with my Savior. Now here's what was even weirder: I was surrounded by other guys my age who loved the Lord. I mean they pursued Him before there were books talking about doing it. We would get together and have all night prayer meetings and God would show up in the form of the precious Holy Spirit and just love on us and show us things. It was a wonderful time. We would have signs and wonders and confirmations. I quickly found that God longs to commune with us. He loves us. If God's willing to show up and move in the midst of young men, He would show up anywhere.

Many times we held these all night prayer meetings in homes and churches. My friends and I started in the little side stage room that had steps leading up to the stage of the sanctuary of the Scott Depot Christ Fellowship. We would meet every Wednesday in the little side stage room during lunch to pray and seek the Lord. The Lord told us dates and locations where we were to meet and pray. The first four all-nighters were at various homes and one other church. These were our faith steps 1 through 4, but God had plans to invite us to higher ground.

After our fourth all-nighter the Lord spoke to me and said, "Ask Pastor Rod if you could have the church sanctuary at Scott Depot Christ Fellowship for an all night prayer meeting."

Now Pastor Rod is a wonderful man of God and at that time was the principal of our Christian school too. The school was in the church facilities.

The sanctuary was so beautiful, ornate, and large so this felt like a huge ask for me as a young teenager. I was very intimidated to ask this man for permission for a group of teenagers to be in this building praying all night. You can imagine the responsibility for me and for Pastor Rod.

Pastor Rod's secretary found me a few hours later in English Class and passed me a note that said, "We pray the Fire Falls." The prayer meeting was on and we would take the high ground of step number 5.

I look back and think of the faith this man had in us to say "Yes" to this request. I can only think that God Himself told him to release us and trust us in this mission.

As we were at the fifth all-nighter in the Scott Depot sanctuary, the Lord spoke to me from the stage and I walked down the 5 steps to the little place where we squeezed into every Wednesday. The Lord showed me that every step from that little room corresponded with a place that He sent us. It's an amazing story of the places we prayed and the things that transpired in those meetings.

Additionally, I saw that every obedience leads to another obedience and another place so that you go higher and your heart becomes more tender to the Holy Spirit and your ear to the voice of God. The other thing we experience in the midst of obedience is JOY. It's Joy Unspeakable and Full of Glory! Rev. Loran Helm taught me that when you obey God, Joy floods into your heart and welcomes a wonderful peace inside your heart. Joy is as the Bible says, "Your Strength." We literally become stronger while we trust God and obey Him on bigger and bigger assignments. Each step represented each place where the guys and I had been shown to pray. As we obeyed, the next step was revealed. The fifth place, the Scott Depot Christ Fellowship sanctuary with its grand, ornate structure, represented the pinnacle of our prayer journey at the time.

It really was a metaphor for what the Lord was showing us. That obedience leads to greater and greater things. My obedience started in a humble room at the Scott Depot Christ Fellowship and has brought me greater assignments including leading groups of people to Israel. Taking believers on a pilgrimage to Israel is an amazing blessing which ushers in an intimacy with the Lord on a new level. The Lord said, "It will be a pilgrimage and I will deal with people in different spots around my Holy Land." That all came from simply hearing the Lord at 15 and Him telling me to get the guys together for prayer. Is it conventional wisdom for a principal to say yes to a young man of 15 with a request to have this church to pray in with his friends with no adult supervision? Probably not. Did it make sense in today's world that young men would desire to seek God and that the Lord would have us to gather in this lovely church? Probably not. But God often doesn't work along the lines of conventional wisdom.

I remember the last time I was heading to Israel and I was sitting on the plane and we had gone quite a distance. I believe we were just flying over the middle of the Atlantic Ocean and I had not felt any stir and I really did not feel much excitement for the trip. I prayed but felt nothing. So I just told the Lord, "I'm gonna watch a movie. You know where I am."

Leading a trip to Israel is a huge responsibility and I take it very seriously that people believe me when I say the Lord has instructed me to go to the Holy Land. I try to stay open to the voice of the Lord. This time after leaving the States I heard and felt nothing. No voice of the Spirit of God. So we walk by faith right? The Lord stirred within me about a few scriptures and I was sharing a few things with those around me. Then I looked at the map that shows the location of the plane. What I saw was the icon of the plane and just behind the plane was "GREECE."

The Lord instantly spoke to my heart and said, "I will always speak to you and lead you beyond the realm of Logic and Reason. Somehow, I saw the map and understood. The plane had passed GREECE which is the birthplace of our logic and reason of men. Now that the plane had flown past GREECE, the Lord was ready to start speaking to me about the trip and at the same time gave me a lesson. To follow the voice of the Lord and do what He says no matter how odd or how much logic or reason is challenged.

The Lord's voice in a person's life is a treasure. The Lord spoke to me the first time when I was around 5 years old. He said, "If you will look up to me, I will always be with you and guide you." My mother, Pat Gidley, told me when I was older that when she was pregnant with me that the Lord spoke to her. She was 6 months along with me and the Lord said, "The child you're carrying belongs to me and I will use him in my Kingdom."

My Father was a rock solid guy. What he said he meant and he always followed through. I never had a problem believing God because I had such an amazing example in Carl Gidley. When my Dad said something, I could "take it to the bank" as they say. Well, he also disciplined me and taught me to obey quickly without delay.

This was a valuable blessing because I was so accustomed to obeying my parents quickly that when the Lord started to give me assignments I simply obeyed.

I will abruptly park here on this thought for a moment. Parents, you have a responsibility to help your children understand obedience and that it must be done quickly. It will cause them to follow and fall in line with the assignment that God has for them. Also we are talking about eternal things. God deals in eternity. Rev. Loran Helm taught me that what God begins never ends. It's like throwing a stone into a lake and seeing the wake go on and on. When we obey God and yield to His voice, it begins a chain reaction in our lives and the lives of those being affected and who will be affected in a glorious and eternal way.

I heard the call of God upon my life formally while at a youth camp in St. Louis, Missouri in 1984. My youth group from the Maranatha Fellowship had met several other youth groups and we had a blast doing Bible quizzes. If I remember correctly, we covered the book of Romans. We won the trophy. On one of the nights, my Pastor James Wright was preaching and he started to call out names of the famous women of God. He prayed out, "Lord, out of these girls give us another Aimee Semple McPherson."

He continued by praying out some other famous
women's names. Then he called out several men
of God from the past, "Lord, give us another Billy
Sunday; Give us another Billy Graham." Then He
called out a name. My heart was pounding. It
was as if the Holy Spirit pulled me over to the
side of the road and was arresting me. Like a
Heavenly Police Officer, He mirandized me on the
spot, "You have a right to remain silent." Then I
heard the Holy Spirit fall on me and say, "Accept
your Calling!"

That night was amazing and as God had it, my
parents were on that trip as youth counselors.
Some would think this would be difficult to be
on a trip like this with your parents, but, my Dad
being sensitive to the issue, just prayed over our
family. He asked the Lord to blind them, my
parents, to me and me to them. It worked. (Once
in a while, I would have to check to see if they
were still around just to be sure. A quick glimpse
was all I required.)

It seemed I never saw my parents (unless I
REALLY cared to) and it gave me that sense of
independence that a kid craves at that time of life.
However, that night when I walked the grassy
aisle to kneel at a picnic bench, I received the
call of God on my life. I could feel the weight of
my Father's Hand on my back as He was there to

pray with me to be commissioned into the service of the Lord. I am deeply thankful that my Father and Mother were there that night to witness this event.

Looking back from 50 to when I was 13, it's clear that the Call upon my life is to inspire people the way I have been inspired. My calling is to cause a desire in people to obey God: To walk in faith and believe Him for everything. To model and remind that He is good and merciful. That He has a plan and even though one might feel lost or directionless, He is with us. We must hold on to the Word.

This chapter is the longest in the book because it's the foundation. Why? When a man puts his whole family in a van to travel to literally only God knows where and to be able to receive from this book, one first must understand that at the onset of this dramatic transition, the Lord had already been speaking to me for over 35 years with confirmation and fruit. I know His voice. The Bible says that His sheep know His Voice. I have had fruit that abounds and multiple confirmations of the Lord speaking and leading us through the years.

After youth camp, my life would consist of prayer, Bible reading, going to school, and playing sports. Most of life was normal. However, I had a passion for the things of God. God began to move in my life in an unusual way. God was teaching me that I could trust Him and that He would provide. Speaking of provision: my friend, Daniel Holstein, and I were going to play tennis and we had our rackets and began to walk to the courts which were a couple miles away and it was before either of us were driving. We were talking of the things of God. Specifically, we were talking of the latest prayer meeting and what He did in the lives of those boys. Suddenly, we arrived at the tennis court.

Then Daniel looked at me and said, "Dude? You got any balls?" We both just laughed because NO I did not and it was OK. We walked all that way with the rackets but NO BALLS!!! LOL! We decided to go ahead because the court was in view. Sit down and rest and then go back. Yet, the Lord GOD had a surprise for us. When we arrived on the court, there were two brand new Wilson tennis balls sitting on the court. It wasn't like somebody was playing and left them. They were placed there beside each other with the Wilson logo facing up so we could see it.

We laughed! We rejoiced. Daniel still has those tennis balls in his office almost 40 years later. What was God saying? This kid must know that I am a Provider. He gave Abraham a ram in the thicket and He gave me two brand new tennis balls. All to show that He can provide the smallest and largest of all we require. He is amazing! Whatever the plan He has for you, you can choose to not be burdened by the weight of your own supply. He has what you require and when you require it. He is Jehovah-Jireh!!! He doesn't know how to fail. Remember, He isn't a respecter of persons. What He has done for one, He will do for all. It's all available if you learn to walk by faith and not by sight.

This is why when the Lord said, "You're outta here in 60 days," I knew that voice and its familiar call. I knew that an adventure was ahead and that all had been provided. He had provided the tennis balls. Now what was He gonna do?

Diving into the Word

As the Lord was preparing us to leave everything to follow where He would lead, I began to dive into the Word of God. It wasn't a decision in my head but in my heart. When I say that I began to be hungry and thirsty for the Word of God, I couldn't get enough. Again, I didn't know what the Lord was going to do with us. But, in hindsight I can say that the Lord was like a trainer taking an athlete and getting rid of the extra weight and filling us with nutrition. We loaded on the Carbs of promise and revelation that would take us the distance in dry places and give us the ability to climb the mountains like a cyclist in the Tour DeFrance.   He was building us up in our most Holy Faith. I devoured the Word of God. It would be nothing to read 10 or 15 chapters at a sitting.

Most of the Scriptures that would come to my attention had to do with Faith. It had to do with the promises that we have in Christ. Seeing things in the Word through the Stories. We saw anew that God sent the Children of Israel out of Egypt fully whole and without sickness. He also provided through the Egyptians the spoil that would eventually provide for the building of the Tabernacle of God — His place upon the Earth. He was showing me that His people could walk through the wilderness without sickness and without lack.

This is a challenge and I find that if we can't measure our experience with what the Word of God says we try to rationalize the Word or reform our beliefs. We see in the lives of those like Smith Wigglesworth, A.A. Allen and others, a supernatural power for miracles, for provision and coming to a place of fullness in the Spirit. A place of belief in what God has said that it actually will manifest in the physical.

Sadly, a part of the church has moved away from the supernatural. When I visit churches, even those that call themselves full Gospel or Spirit-filled churches, they sing, they preach and take offerings but they don't minister to people at the altar. The laying on of hands has gone the way of the dinosaur. Some don't even give an altar call. We have guys that talk and chat in the pulpit who sometimes make us laugh or feel good. But we lack an encounter that comes with Holy Ghost conviction, that sorrow that is Godly that makes a man desire to submit to God. We ought to long for His life giving power: the Spirit falling upon a person that causes them to fall to the floor or as some call it slain in the Spirit.

Here's a helpful analogy: When you go to a hospital for an operation, they don't tell you to stand there while they cut you open and take care of the problem. You first must lie down then they give you anesthesia and cut ya open and go to work. Likewise, when the Spirit of God comes upon somebody at the altar and it's genuine, they often fall down and seem to be in a trance or asleep or they may be laughing under the 'anesthesia' of the Spirit. God is going in by His Spirit and changing the wiring, healing the rejection, and taking out the results of abuse via supernatural surgery.

I have seen the very thought patterns of people changed under the power of God. For you computer geeks, it's like getting an upgrade of your software. We were made to operate by the power and Spirit of God. We do not operate correctly while in the flesh. So, be careful not to judge the tears at the altar or the falling down or the rolling around on the ground. Sometimes you'll even hear the noises or the moans of the Spirit which is completely scriptural. Men in the presence of God become as Dead but for His mercy. I found that in my prayer closet that God was carving me into what He desired me to be and cleansing my heart. The Word of God was growing in my heart. The 'software upgrade' was causing a change of thinking, processing, and causing me to understand more of God and what His purpose was for my Life.

God's Observation Deck

When I speak of Observation, I am speaking of God having me take my iPad into my prayer closet and He would take me to Youtube or Vimeo and I would observe men of God and their teaching. I would listen to Kenneth Hagen do a healing school in the '50's or see Oral Roberts preach about the 4th Man in the Fire. I would see Charles Capps go after doubt and fear. I would see Kenneth Copeland talk of becoming a partner with Oral Roberts for $10.00 a month and that gave him access to the same grace or ability that Oral operated in for ministry. Don't think it strange when Paul said that the Philippians were partakers of his grace because of their support for His ministry.

Bottom Line: Faith Comes by Hearing. Technology has given us the ability to defile ourselves or build ourselves up. A POD is what? Something that has seeds in it. An iPod is something that has seeds in it. Get IT? GET IT? When you see people with their Ear Buds in their ears, consider what is Budding in their mind. What seeds are they planting? You can now listen to the most amazing anointed sermons at a moment's notice. We are not able to attend healing school with Kenneth Hagen in person. He has passed to his reward. But, you can listen to the recordings and watch videos and simply enjoy the word that builds your faith.

I have experienced the same power that I experienced from Rodney Howard Browne's meetings coming through my iPad the same as when I was there in the front row. What are we planting in our minds? What truly is the music planting in our head and spirit? We must take an account of the spiritual nutrition that is coming into our souls.

I found that when I read the Word and climbed up onto the Observation Deck to hear the voices of God's Servants both past and present, the seed began to germinate on the inside of me. It was causing my faith to build. Who can listen to Kathryn Kuhlman and not desire to know the Holy Spirit more? Who can hear Kenneth Hagen without knowing that God is the same yesterday, today and forever? Can you listen to Reinhard Bonnke without having a fire for the souls of men? See what I mean? God is the author of these technologies. I recently heard Kenneth Copeland say that he had 27 translations of the Word on His phone. So can you! So can you do what I did and carve out time and watch preaching and let your faith grow by HEARING what the Spirit is saying?

I encourage you to get into the Word and climb up on to the Observation Deck and behold the transformation in your thinking and processing of Life. Watch ideas in business and ministry begin to bud because of what is budding in your spirit by the seeds you are planting by your eyes and ears.

It's a great day and I invite you to enter in and camp in the shadow of His wing! Now for us, the cloud had moved upward which was our signal to start packing up the camp.

GENESIS 12:1

Now the Lord had said unto Abram, Get thee out of thy country, and from thy kindred, and from thy father's house, unto a land that I will shew thee:

CHAPTER 3

Time to Launch Out Into the DEEP

I have always had Grace from God to simply obey Him. I guess it just made sense to me. Obviously God had used the stories that I previously told you to build my faith and to show that He had the ability to provide and lead me. Now that the rubber was meeting the road, I had lunch with my wife, Sabrina, to tell her what the Lord had told me. Turns out she already knew that God was taking us somewhere. My kids knew that God was taking us to another place. We all knew it was geographical and simultaneously we knew it was spiritual. It was time to take that unimaginable step of faith!

We called for a POD to fill with our belongings. We sold many things during that 60 day period of time and the things that we desired to keep we put in storage. Our 60 days were filled with Joy—

the Joy you can only experience when you begin to separate yourself from the things of the world and prepare to Launch out into the Deep. My heart understood Peter when he called to the Lord and said, "Bid me come." He longed to experience the impossible; he was willing to leave his comfort zone. The time with Jesus stirred him to desire something MORE. However, the future was vague. We didn't have much of a schedule and we didn't have much money either. At the time, we only had one meeting on the books for early April with our friends in Tennessee.

I understood; my family understood. We had beautiful weather that final week we were in Aiken, SC to load the POD. It was easy and it was wonderful. Just knowing we were getting ready to go on an adventure like this. The other miracle was that I had just returned from Israel 14 days earlier. Normally, it can take 2 weeks just to feel a bit normal again after a trip where you walk for 50 miles and get up when you're normally going to bed. But the Grace and Ability of God was upon me and my strength was surprisingly normal as we packed up a house and loaded our belongings.

The last night in the house, we slept in sleeping bags. I tell ya, as I'm writing this right now, I'm shaking my head and smiling thinking probably what you're thinking. WHAT AN IDIOT!!! I mean leave everything?? Believe me the thought had crossed my mind. However, I knew that I knew that God was the author of this story and that He desired to show His ability to lead and guide our steps.

The last night sleeping on the floor with my kids felt like a campout. But when the next morning came my first thought when I woke up was, "WHERE ARE WE SLEEPING TONIGHT?"

The morning we left wasn't a glorious morning - it was April and rainy and cold. I have joked with people and said I had a cardboard sign underneath my seat just in case we ended up in a Walmart parking lot with nothing that would say "Will Work For Food." I wish I could say LOL, but my heart and my senses were in a deep place of "HMMMMMMM...what next?" But God would stir my faith with reminding me of scriptures like:

> *Philippians 4:19 - "My God shall supply all of my needs according to His riches in Glory by Christ Jesus."*

> *Hebrews 13:5b - "I will never leave thee nor forsake thee."*

> *Philippians 4:13 - "I can do all things through Christ who strengthens me."*

Fortunately, I had the Word of God on the inside and I was accessing it. We can't start looking up promises when the plane is going down. We must have the Word on the inside of us. Link our faith to what God said in His Word and access it by Faith. All supply is in His Grace. Paul said in Romans 5:2, "I have access by faith into this Grace."

The hand of faith reaches into His riches. His Grace supplies our every need. It was there from the beginning of time. Everything has been set aside for everything that we will require in this lifetime. No matter the situation as you read this, your provision was set aside for you before the need arose. God isn't on His throne perplexed and tapping His forehead saying, "WOW, didn't see this one coming." LOL!

We never were without or not supplied for and we never camped out broke at Walmart. We stopped at many Walmarts but we were always fully supplied and lacking nothing. TIME to Launch out into the Deep!

PSALM 18:46

The LORD liveth; and blessed be my rock; and let the God of my salvation be exalted.

CHAPTER 4

Upon This Rock

Since we had a few days to meander before our only scheduled meeting in Tennessee, we decided to head south to visit our friends at WBPI TV 49 Watchman Broadcasting . As I mentioned before, the day we left, April 9th 2018, was a day I will never forget. It wasn't like the previous week which was sunny and beautiful and when we felt at peace with our decision. The weather had turned rainy and cold as we were cramming the last bits of our earthly goods into our van on top of our children. The atmosphere shift was noticeable! Fear was knocking on the door, but we didn't dare answer.

We were basically homeless by choice. We were leaving to go where God was going to lead us. I gotta take a minute and brag on my wife and say, "What a woman!" She was willing to leave everything that seemed logical and normal to follow this man, her husband, into this adventure of trusting God and seeing what He does with us.

We stopped by the local Christian television station, Watchman TV, which is led by Russell and Dorothy Spaulding. They walk an amazing walk of faith: Carrying the Cross literally up and down highways and by-ways ministering to whomever the Lord puts in their way. They had opened that station to us and had put us on the show. We sang and ministered for months and had a great time. We wanted to say goodbye and we wanted to have prayer. They were gracious with us and then placed a $500.- seed into our ministry.

It was a surprise blessing because we were barely 20 miles into our journey when seed had already come into our hands. We left and hit the road I-20 West towards Atlanta. There were a couple of things that were on my heart for a few weeks as far as direction goes. I had been thinking of Stone Mountain outside of Atlanta. I had never been there but I had seen something on the news regarding the beautiful Civil War Monument that had been designed into the Rock, much like Mount Rushmore. I felt a pull to go there. We didn't know much about it but we knew it was on the way to Nashville.

As we went toward Atlanta, the weather improved and we found Stone Mountain. It turned out to be a beautiful place for families. We decided to stay there that night and tour the area the next day. When we awoke that next day, we found that we could take a cable car to the top and get onto this impressive piece of granite Rock. We got to the top and it was so clear you could see Atlanta and several other towns from the top. We talked to one couple at the top who said, "We have been up here several times but it's always cloudy or foggy. We have never seen it this clear."

So needless to say we were thankful for that report. I found a place all to myself and started to ponder our direction: where were we headed next? I was praying and I heard the Holy Spirit say these words to me, "My covenant with you is stronger and larger than this Stone Mountain."

I was stunned. A peace and assurance came over me. I finally knew why God had brought us to this place called Stone Mountain. He wanted to show me something: while it looked as if I was homeless and defenseless, He was my foundation and His promises weren't just words. They were a binding covenant that my family and I could stand on and believe. We could launch into this journey knowing that we could stand upon this Rock.

Sabrina came to me and said, "I want you to sing 'On Christ The Solid Rock I Stand.' "

Even though I'm a singer, I'm not one of those that is just dying for attention and have the attitude of "look what I can do." LOL But she was very persuasive and I
began to sing and a few people gathered and stopped as I sang.

On Christ the solid Rock I stand,

All other ground is sinking sand,

All other ground is sinking sand.

We left that place knowing that we had had a Bethel type experience. God had met us. We were standing on Christ, standing on His promises and that those promises were and are true.

I encourage you today as you read this....Launch out into what God has called you to do. Have the courage to show your faith! Walk in Faith. Live by Faith. He is your foundation and that foundation is sure. It is an Immovable Rock upon which is an unshakable Kingdom. There's a song that Sandi Patti made famous called "Upon This Rock," the music which was composed by our dear friend, Dony McGuire.

Upon this Rock, I'll build my kingdom,
Upon this Rock forever and ever it shall stand.
Upon this Rock of Revelation I'll build a strong
and mighty nation.
And it shall stand the storms of time
upon this rock.

That Rock is Christ.
By Him and For Him were all things made.

One of my favorite places in all of Israel is
Caesarea Philippi, the place where Jesus asked His
disciples, "Whom do men say that I am?" Unless
you're there, you can't understand the gravity.
This was a hard and wicked location filled with
all kinds of temples and human sacrifice. A cave
where sacrifices of all sorts were thrown into
the cave and they would look for the blood in
the river that ran from the cave as a sign of the
sacrifice being accepted. This cave has been given
the name, The Gates of Hell. So when Jesus said,
"and the gates of Hell will not prevail against it."
What did He mean? Against what? The Church
built upon the Rock. What Rock? The Rock is the
revelation. That Jesus is the Christ, the son of the
living God.

Leaving Stone Mountain, I knew that I stood
upon the Rock of Revelation, Jesus the Christ. He
was with us, within us and we within Him. What
a Rock of Revelation!

I SAMUEL 15:22

And Samuel said,
Hath the Lord as great
delight in burnt offerings and
sacrifices, as in obeying the
voice of the Lord?
Behold, **to obey is better**
than sacrifice*, and to*
hearken than the fat of rams.

CHAPTER 5

A New Season

Many people talk of a new season - a time when new things could begin to happen. Or it could be a previous vision or desire that could come to pass in their lives. But they just talk about it and never really experience it. Some people are satisfied with simply talking about a new season and taking no action. I have heard people talk this way and I'm sure you have also.

When someone says, "I've been thinking about doing _____ for the Kingdom," my first reaction is to respond with, "How long will you disobey God?" How long will one strive between two opinions? People either obey or do not obey God. There is no in-between.

We will never experience the power of the new season until we obey and step into that new season. The power of the new season is IN the new season - not talking of a new season but stepping into that new season. Obedience is BETTER than sacrifice. Obedience is the key that unleashes the power and presence of God. It sets things into motion. This is where the statement you are not waiting on God, God is waiting upon you applies.

The Gidley family could have talked about leaving. We could have practiced it or rehearsed it. But to get to that next season required action on our part as believers of the Word. When God said, "You're outta here in 60 days," we began to take action. Right then was when the next season's power was released. Many stand in a stale lifeless former place of wonder looking over into what might be possible. All they would require is to simply take action. Obey what God said. My purpose in writing our story is to help people leave the perch of human observation. Jump into what God is telling you to do. Launch out into the deep. I love that statement! My good friend, John Mason, always signs his books that way and it always stirs me. The catch isn't on shore - it's out there beneath the waves of challenge and impossibility.

When we arrived in Nashville or specifically Springfield, TN to Dr. Arlin Smith's home, we didn't know that we had already leapt into the new season with power. We were significantly more than we were before because our obedience to the word from God had opened a door. An anointing had been released. We arrived at the small apartment that they have on their property. Dr. Arlin told us that this was our home as long as we desired and whenever we were in the area we could have it. He prayed for us and he specifically prayed over my wife. She immediately felt strengthened. We planned to have a Sunday of meetings. These were our first meetings since leaving everything and going on the road. That Sunday morning was so powerful. People were touched and the power and presence of our mighty God was in our midst. That Sunday night Dr. Arlin spoke to me and asked, "Can we continue these meetings??"

I said, "Sure!" I knew God desired it.

I have had hundreds of Sundays in my ministry. This was the first time that a Pastor had asked us to stay and continue the meetings because the Spirit's power was so strong. I realized that was the first sign of the new season. One meeting turned into a week of seeking His presence and blending with this wonderful congregation. The provision was amazing from this congregation also. Dr. Arlin was amazed at the giving of his congregation and it was an amazing blessing as a door had opened in NYC. We were blessed with the finances in abundance to go and do what God had said to go and do.

Obey God. Do what He has placed in your heart. Provision and Help are before you.

GENESIS 6:22

Thus did Noah; according to all that God commanded him, so did he.

CHAPTER 6

The Ark Experience

In the days and weeks prior to leaving South Carolina, I had a few places and destinations that came up in my heart. One of those places was in Kentucky, The Ark Experience, the life size replica of Noah's Ark. Ken Ham is an apologetics expert and the visionary of the The Ark Experience and the Creation Museum. It was just in my heart to get to these places. I didn't have any connections in that area, but I knew that I desired to take my children, Maximus, Giselle and Gabriella, to these places.

This world is gunning for our children and we have to teach our kids why we believe what we believe. "Because I said so" or "That's what Grandpa said" isn't going to discourage them from listening to the world. To be able to give a wise and accurate account of why we believe what we believe and why we believe the Bible is vitally important. I knew we were supposed to go, but again we had no real connection to anything else in the area.

It's funny how God will put a little light in your heart; something that you can't shake. Sometimes it's a location or a trip you should take. Maybe a city or just a little something in your heart. That is God putting something inside your spirit. A direction and destination. Well, I had that prompting with this trip to Kentucky. I just put it in the Lord's hands and said, "I will go."

A few years ago I was on the phone with a wonderful Pastor by the name of Byron Mills. We had a wonderful time on the phone and God had given me a very accurate word for him in the season he was in, but he never felt the leading of the Lord to have me come to the church. It just wasn't the time.

When we launched into the new season, new doors began to open. Timing changes things and opportunities start to present themselves. We were taking a few days in Springfield, TN at Dr. Arlin's property. I was sitting in the living room when Facebook Messenger beeped. I looked and it was Pastor Byron asking me to come to the church as fast as possible within the next few weeks. After years of wondering about why there was no open door, all of a sudden here was an invitation. We prayed together over the dates and the Lord put a weekend in May of 2018 in our hearts which was just about 5 weeks after leaving South Carolina on this remarkable Journey.

The weekend we were at Pastor Byron's church in Kentucky was graduation Sunday. Pastor Byron said he had so many kids and graduates in his church that he would never have anytime with us. But, he agreed that this was the time that the Lord directed us there.

We can never go by logic and reason when walking with God. I don't mean that we resort to being stupid or reckless. There is nothing wreckless about God including His Love but that is another story, LOL. God is a God of order. However, more often than not, what God says to do is going to crucify your flesh and cause your mind to wonder about what we are doing. That is where faith comes in and we simply do our best to obey what the Holy Spirit says to do to the best of our ability.

Let me free up your mind with a perspective on obedience. **We're going to miss it. We will flub up.** We're gonna look at the winds and the waves instead of looking at Jesus, just like Peter did. We're going to go left when we should have gone right. But God already knew that we would mess up and has made provision for us. We aren't able to "bat 1000" and God isn't worried about it. We shouldn't worry either.

The Western way or Greek way of thinking is extremely linear versus the Hebrew way of thinking which is more circular. Growing up in the Western Culture which came to us from Greek philosophy and thinking we see things very linear. Meaning we see things as building blocks or A to Z. You can't get to B unless you go through A. There's no way you can get to D without successfully navigating C. This is very difficult to live by because we all make mistakes. It's something that produces a people who are living under a huge weight of condemnation. Some think, "I messed up early in life and cannot get to the plan that God has for me." Now with my love for the Jewish people and the culture, I have seen something beautiful. They see life as going in cycles. Remember the Bible says He is the wheel within the wheel.

Our seasons run in cycles: a circular motion. If you have a rotten summer, don't worry, another one is coming along. The pattern of the last 6,000 years isn't broken. As the song says, "The sun'll come out, tomorrow."

In life God has done something wonderful. He already knew that we would mess up, so He provided Jesus as our Savior. He also has provided the cycle of life. He knew that we would mess up in this summer or winter of life. But He will uses it to mature us and bring us to the next place so that we can succeed and get it right.

The beautiful thing is that God hasn't set us up to fail. He has set us up to grow and mature and to be transformed to get it right. You wonder if God has this ability. Ever heard that Jesus was slain before the foundation of the world? Yes, but He died in Jerusalem didn't He? Yes He did, however, He died before the foundation. Before we failed, before we were born, He had provided for our forgiveness and, yes, our success.

Once we fail, the only way to stay in failure is to quit. Realize that Christ is our Kinsman redeemer. He makes it right. He has made the way. So we keep our Chins UP and Knees DOWN. The devil is an accuser of the brethren but God has set up the seasons and the cycles and given Jesus as our Savior.

Back to our decision making process, God simply loves that we are taking action to the best of our ability to follow Him. He is a good Father. He loves you and is not looking to hurt you or humiliate you. Did you get upset when your child fell down when trying to walk? No, of course not. You helped the little cutie up and then started again. You were thrilled they desired to walk and explore the world. Our Father is the same way. Just trust Him and His love for you.

Upon arriving in Maysville, KY, we went to Pastor Byron's church. Pastor Byron was not there to greet us ahead of time. He had warned us that he was going to be having a very busy Sunday. Well, that was designed by God. I stood up that morning and began sing. I sang a few songs and then began to speak. The prophetic word began to come from my heart. This was a general word that God had tailored for their congregation. But then God started to have me address different people from the congregation. I began to speak over them and as I did their eyes would fill with tears and some would fall under the power of the Spirit. This happened with several people. Then I looked over and Pastor Byron had his face in his hands. The power of God was all over him.

God obviously brought us there to deal with some very sensitive things. Also, He brought us in at a very busy time so that we wouldn't talk and the Pastor couldn't be accused of giving me information. God was so good to reveal His will and bring all things to light to help bring this church to a closer place of oneness and agreement.

We left after the service and noticed that we were now only an hour away from The Ark Experience and The Creation Museum.

I didn't know why it had been placed in my heart to go to The Ark Experience. But, I knew that it was essential to get there. When it settled upon me, I had no way of being able to make it come to pass but as we simply followed and obeyed God, the pieces began to come together and now I found myself heading towards the Ark.

Noah was an amazing guy. He built the Ark in the middle of a situation where nobody would understand what in the world he was doing. Man, did I get that after seeing the Ark in Kentucky and experiencing the power of God in Pastor Byron's church. God really desired for me to look to Him alone. There were some people that I didn't even tell what we were doing. I just didn't wish to be looked at with that stare of "What are you doing?" or "How can you do that (travel all over creation) with children?" That always seemed a strange thing to say to me as if children were a burden of some sort. I was doing that FOR my children. I was obeying God to the best of my ability. I desired for my kids to see their Mom and me stepping out for right or for wrong. Let's go for it and not just sit.

The Bible is full of great stories. I love the lepers from 2 King 7:3 just looking at each other and saying, "Why sit we here till we die? LET'S MOVE!!!" I hear people say that God is dealing with them or speaking to them to do this or that. Later on they are still speaking the same thing and nothing has changed. That is delay. Delayed obedience is disobedience! Do it. Do what He said!

At the time I heard from God that we were leaving South Carolina, we were living in a leased house. Upon speaking with my wife, Sabrina, she confirmed the desire to obey God with me. We called the real estate company and put in our notice that we were leaving. WHY? Because we knew God had spoken. To show our faith meant we ought to act, to move, to proceed by faith and that would activate the process. Faith brings the provision from the unseen to the seen. We had to act.

We had a glorious time learning apologetics from the Creation Museum and then we went to the Ark. The size of the Ark was amazing. 500 ft long. So wide and three decks. The engineering and specific process that it required to make this thing. An astonishing 120 year walk of faith for Noah.

Later in the day when the crowds had dwindled down, my family of five was walking around on the inside of this enormous vessel. It hit me that Noah had 8 people and we felt the enormous task Noah had of building and then believing that God would fill the Ark and then the animals would come, and then it would rain. Then they were floating over turbulent waters and Noah's family was tossed about for a long time all because God said so. I was amazed at Noah's stamina and his leadership to get his family to come along on this journey. While standing on the inside of the Ark, I got it. God was using this physical expression of the Ark to help me understand that Noah's faith to believe God was what I had to do. We were on a journey that was way outta our comfort zone. We really didn't know what in the world we were doing and where we were going. But we knew God had us on this journey. I thought maybe it would last 90 days or so. It turned out to be 441 days of miracles and following. God also was in the process of getting things fixed and worked out as we began this journey. When we obey God, we give Him access into everything that is ours and that is us. He will work in our minds and hearts. He will fix wounds from the past and prepare us for the future that He has planned.

Our time in the Ark was an unforgettable experience. It kinda centered me and helped me to understand that we really were on a faith journey. Noah didn't know where the Ark would land and I had no idea where we were gonna sleep the next night. But God was making the way. I knew that God had placed the Ark in my heart so our kids could experience it too. Now I know that God was directing us to the Ark. It felt as if He sealed us and shut the big door and we were really on our way. I was so moved by my experience at the Ark that I got my picture taken in front of the grand door of the Ark. You'll see that photo on the cover of my CD titled "This is My Surrender" which is available on our website crownvoiceministries.com. The Ark Experience was a direct metaphor for our experience. Time to continue the journey!!!

2 Corinthians 3:18

But we all, with open face beholding as in a glass the glory of the Lord, are changed into the same image from **glory to glory***, even as by the Spirit of the Lord.*

CHAPTER 7

Glory TO Glory

There are many lessons that we learned upon this trip. I found that out as we stepped into this next season. My whole family began to change. Gifts and abilities began to manifest in each of the five members of our family. The Word says that we go from Glory **TO** Glory. It's that "TO" that will get ya. It's a small word but it implies huge challenges. When we're walking by faith, we must constantly remind ourselves of the Word. It truly is a sword - it is a weapon. It reminds us of what God has said and that we must get really stubborn when it comes to believing this Word. I must decide within myself and make a decision that I am going to GO with God. That I am willing to MOVE. Many times in certain churches as I minister in the Lord, He will prompt me to ask the crowd, "Do you want a move of God?" People will say "Yes!" or raise their hands and agree. Then I'll say, "Really? Then pick up your things and move. Right now. Go to another section of this church. Go sit somewhere you have never sat before." You would be amazed at the attitudes that arise and sometimes you would be amazed at the Joy that comes. If you can't move physically to another pew or row without a problem, then you're going to have a problem with God's call. I challenge people. I desire for people to think. Find another way to work. Find another grocery store to shop in. Go to another place for dinner. Be different. Don't get into a ditch. God is about change and transforming us from Glory TO Glory and that requires growing and letting God stretch us.

One of the changes was in my wife, Sabrina. When we first got married and we would travel, she would say a few words to the church then sit down. Sometimes she would perform one of her amazing ballet performances. During our years together, she had developed into a great speaker and had spoken in various places for ladies groups. However, something was different and very pristine in Sabrina as we put on the miles and ministered and drove.

I really noticed it when Pastor Arlin Smith called me a little before Mother's Day in 2018 and said, "Hey, can you come for Mothers Day?"

I said, "Sure, we're on our way to Florida. It would be great to stop in and see you. We could stay a day or two at the apartment while I minister and then we'll hit the road again."

But then he said, "That all sounds great, but, I want Sabrina to speak, not you." LOL!

I said, "I'll ask her."

She said, "Yes." I was thrilled. I know what is in my wife and I know her desire to communicate the gospel of Christ.

The day came and she got up. She told me before she went on stage that she probably had 10 minutes worth of speaking and asked me to be ready to sing or take over at that point.

Well, Sabrina took the stage and about 45 to 50 min later she was still preaching and stomping her foot into the ground and sharing what was in her heart. It was amazing and I just sat there with my mouth open wondering, "Who is this woman that was before me?" She was changing from Glory TO Glory and Faith TO Faith. It was awesome and fun! This continued to happen on our journey into New Mexico, California and many other places where I have seen God use Sabrina in a powerful way.

Again, isn't it amazing that God will open opportunities for Himself to shine through you? Yet we feel like we don't have enough. God works through weakness. I believe in being prepared and doing your study. However, I can't tell you how many times that I have stood up with notes and God took me over like a hand in a glove and spoke the wonders of the Gospel just the way people required to hear it. Nowadays I actually just enjoy my Saturday and pray and prepare but I rarely have many notes. Too many notes make for a speech which may not be something that is truly anointed. I now write bullet points of my thoughts and things that the Lord gives me. Yet, sometimes that isn't what God brings out. Now after 20 years, most of the time I just try to stay in fellowship with the precious Holy Spirit and let Him bring out what He is going to bring. This method isn't for everyone, but for my ministry and what God has called me to do, I can't "get up in my head" with what I ought to do. I've gotta let the Lord lead in the moment. I gotta stay prayed up, studied up, fueled up and be ready to be used by God.

I found on our journey that Max also began to hear the voice of the Lord. I remember in Paso Robles, CA on the way to church Maximus said, "Dad, I just heard the Lord speak to me and say......!"

It was a message for the precious church that we were ministering in at that time. I let Max come up at a specific time in the service and share the word for the church and it lit up the meeting.

My youngest daughter who was 5 at the time was in a service and went down to the floor to start to color. Normally, she usually just watches me and cuddles with her momma. She enjoys the presence of God and watching Dad. But this instance was during an altar service and a gentleman went back to his seat after we ministered to him. Once this man was seated, Bella went down to the floor and began to color. She colored a picture of Jesus at the cross with a man kneeling down. No big deal for her to color a pretty picture, however that wasn't the end. She pulled on her mom's shirt and said, "The Lord wanted me to draw this picture for this man who is sitting in the back."

Can you imagine the wonder of the God of the Universe speaking to the heart of a little 5 year old to color a picture? Again coloring a picture wasn't hard for little Bella, but what the obedience-breakthrough factor was, was pulling on her momma's shirt and saying, "The Lord told me to take this picture to this man in the back. Will you come with me?"

Well, Sabrina had instant "ice cream eyes." LOL, that is what we call tears in the eyes - like ice cream dripping down a cone on a hot summer day. They went back together and Bella gave the picture to this man. Then he got "ice cream eyes" PTL!

The Pastor told us later on a phone call that that man has had Bella's picture on his refrigerator and sees it everyday and it ministers so much to him. Why? It reminded the man of his time at the altar which was complete surrender to the Cross of Christ and the way he was really supposed to be walking with God. How amazing that God would use a 5-year-old to encourage a man to keep kneeling and following Jesus!

Giselle became a warrior for Christ on this trip. Boldness, Courage!! When she was in Christian School in Riverside, CA (don't worry we will get to that open door that wasn't just for Giselle but Maximus and Bella also), Giselle would lay hands and minister to other girls at the school who were going through things from home. She started to have visions in our meetings and they were powerful. She is still having powerful visions since that time.

For me it is a blessing to see that obedience brings growth. As Noah gathered his family to build the Ark, I could see that I had gathered my family to leave everything and follow Jesus. Remember, I didn't have to convince anybody of this trip. God was dealing with Sabrina and my kids that we were going somewhere soon and to get ready to leave.

The takeaway here is that as we obey God, we will have great JOY. We will also have tremendous growth in our own heart, soul and spirit. We will begin to perceive things that we never thought we could before. We will begin to live in that realm of faith and the unseen. We will begin to realize that He is faithful from beginning to end and that nothing is impossible!

JEREMIAH 32:27

Behold, I am the Lord, the God of all flesh: is there any thing too hard for me?

CHAPTER 8

There and Back Again!!!

Being a *Lord of the Rings* fan I couldn't write this book without mentioning 'There and Back Again' in this book. I also know that writing this book in obedience is "Taking care of business" which was Elvis Presley's slogan. So now that I have used both of those within this book, we can get down to the business of this chapter. I have written mostly a chronological story from the time we left South Carolina and have recalled the first two months on the road. From now on I am going to share with you stories that will build your faith and encourage you to obey God. To obey is better than sacrifice. That really is the reason I use the phrase "There and Back Again" by Bilbo Baggins or in this case Tim Gidley. We went and we came back but we were changed and many other people were changed also. We learned how to use Faith. More than just talk of it, we used it and drew upon the Grace of God for every provision that we required. My oh My, the Joy of watching God provide and change circumstances around. Time and again we walked into what seemed to be a storm. We watched and saw that He still has the ability to speak into the situation as He did on the Sea of Galilee and say "Peace Be Still." We have an amazing God and we have been given the Word.

Many people, especially those who find themselves in the Prophetic or Pentecostal movement, yearn for a special word from the LORD. Well, I understand. Sometimes you desire a personal word from God and God has used me hundreds of times to do just that all over this globe. However, in the midst of all of that, I have found a love and desire to take in the Love Note, the Word of God from Genesis to Revelation. To understand that this is a Word to us in the body. It is a Word to you. When the Bible says "FEAR NOT" 365 times, one for every day of the year, that is exactly what it means.

When it says in the Bible, "Faithful is He that calls you who will also do it," that is a tremendous word! I could tell you by the Spirit that God is faithful and He has put gifts in you to accomplish His will. But HEY Paul beat me to it. LOL!!! The same God that called you is the same God that will work through you. Hand in a glove. We must understand that by the Spirit, God can take words written thousands of years ago and make it relevant to our current situation for our help and for our comfort and instruction.

We see fearless obedience in the first chapter of Joshua!! Be Strong and Courageous. Thank God that wasn't just for Joshua who was still in the desert, had just lost his mentor, and had a few million people looking to him to know what to do next. It is also for us in our situation. We have standing orders to be Strong and Courageous and to have believing faith that God will do what He said He would do. It's just like He told Abraham and it was reviewed by Paul in Romans Chapter 4. Abraham was strongly persuaded that what God had promised He was also able to do.

Another part of the Word of God says, "IS there anything too hard for the Lord?" I hope you get it. Personal words are awesome, but there is a Word that is sitting in your living room now or right beside your bed or thanks to the vision of tech giants is in your phone in about 27 available translations - at least that is how many translations are in Kenneth Copeland's phone. LOL!!!

So, what follow from here on is Non-Fiction glory to God! This isn't a novel: this is real!

A family packed up at the word of the Lord and left Aiken, South Carolina not knowing where they were going. They didn't have a hefty sum. Their Discover Card didn't leave much for them to Discover. LOL!!! It was inconvenient and they didn't know anything except what He said.

God took them over 40,000 miles in a Chrysler Town and Country from State to State and Church to Church, to TV stations and Radio Stations. To Israel and Back and yes finally arriving back in Aiken, South Carolina to start another amazing chapter of events.

I believe now as I feel that Prophetic gift moving in me that God had you buy this book. Maybe I gave it to you during a service while I shared about the book and you were the blessed receiver. But this will go into your spirit and revive things that you thought were dead. The Living Christ will inspire you as He did me with His breath of life. You will find yourself blessed, healed and strengthened. Regarding the things that you have been afraid to do, you will now arise and begin to do. It may be to run for city council, or school board, to leave the current career or job and begin the business that is in your heart.

But you will be filled and no longer empty. Your mind will be swirling with new ideas and you will feel the RIVER of GOD on the inside. Giftings you didn't know you had will come forth and people choose to support and bless you in your endeavors will arrive just in time.

Behold, I set before you an open door that no man can shut!!

MATTHEW 12:37

For by thy words thou shalt be justified, and by thy words thou shalt be condemned.

CHAPTER 9

Whatsoever Things You Desire

My kids love God. They also believe that God is Good. They believe that He is a provider. They believe that God is a speaking Spirit and that we are created in His Image; not just a form, but a likeness. The apple doesn't fall far from the tree. I'm sure you have heard that said many times when referring to how a child looks or acts. People always say that Maximus is a chip off the ol' block. Many say that Giselle has the same features as her mother. I always say, "same model, different paint job" as Sabrina has black hair and tan skin and Giselle is a blonde, green-eyed beauty. However her traits and looks are the same. Bella is the only child that shares her mother's beautiful brown eyes.

Great, Tim, so what's the Point? Our Father is a speaking Spirit. So are we. When He breathed into Adam and he became a living soul, God imparted Himself into Adam. For example, in Genesis 1, we see that the earth was dark, void, and covered in water yet the Spirit of God hovered over it. I always have found this to be very interesting. The Spirit of the Lord was around and over the situation, however, nothing was happening until the Words from the Father LIGHT BE were spoken!!! When He spoke those words, it mixed with the brooding Spirit of the Lord and BOOOOM!! Creation began to take form. I have found by experience and the wisdom of those that have taught me that God is with us and He will never leave us or forsake us. But we have a part to play. Words come from what we think. The Bible in Philippians says to think on THESE things. Whatsoever things are pure, right, lovely and of good report. It's important what you think because it's the loading chamber for the mouth.

Good Report HMMMM. That takes me to the story of the children of Israel coming close to going into the Promised Land. God orders them to go and take the land. However, most of the men were timid. They had heard of the giants of the land. They sent in 12 spies. It says that Joshua and Caleb said, "We are well able to take this land." Yet the other 10 spies gave an *evil report* the Bible says.

The *evil report* is going the opposite direction from what God says to do. It's the Jonah in us that runs the other way and gets into the boat and falls asleep in the bottom. Yet the rebellious action causes a storm. The *evil report* is saying the opposite of what Heaven is saying. If Heaven is saying you can take the land and you doubt and SAY with your mouth the opposite then you are in an *evil report* realm. Remember, the believing of the *evil report* caused a huge delay in going into the Promised Land. A generation of unbelief had to pass. Unbelief is a huge problem in the church and Christian life. You cannot manifest what God has for you if you do not believe the report of the Lord. We will cover more on this later.

This is why Paul said the miracle is in your mouth. Salvation begins by confessing with your mouth and believing in your heart. You can go throughout the Word of God and see that what you say in a situation has much to do with the outcome. Like our Heavenly Father, we must release the words LIGHT BE to see the situation change. The Spirit of the Lord is the Egg and your words are the Seed. Mixed together there is the beginning of Creation.

Whatever you face in this life, the Bible has got it covered. You simply must find a promise that relates to the situation that you are in. Remember that chorus "Give Thanks" which says, "Let the weak SAY [SAY SAY] I am strong. Let the poor SAY [SAY SAY] I am rich." In Proverbs 6:2 it says, "Thou art snared with the words of thy mouth," which means to be caught in a trap and you can't walk out because I love you, too much Baby. (Oh, sorry, an Elvis lyric crept in. LOL you know what I am saying.)

Do all things without murmuring or disputing. This means quit casting a dam in front of what God desires to do in your life. Taking responsibility is key here. Your mom said it best, "WATCH YOUR MOUTH!!!" It's a must. Now I was speaking of my children at the beginning of this chapter. Those things they learned are because we taught them. Also we never shielded our kids from a financial challenge that we had, but as a family we would always take the request to the Heavenly Father. That way when He provides, the kids know it's God. If they didn't know about it previously or weren't allowed to invest their faith into the situation, then they can't really party with us when the provision or answer arrives.

We gotta train our children to believe God for themselves. We must teach them the principles that will allow them to stand in faith when nobody else is around or when we're not around. You may have heard me say this in a meeting. In the future, I might be a Billionaire but if my kids are on the other side of the world and they have a need and I don't have the ability to get provision to them, they must know how to put the Word into use and call on this mighty God who provides. He provided Abraham a ram in the thicket so he didn't have to slay his son, Isaac. He is Jehovah Jireh, Our Provider.

After our family had been living in California for a while, our friends, Jimmy and Becky Pearce, helped us to make contact with a great congregation in Livermore, CA. Yet, when we pulled into town, we were tired and on top of this we didn't have much money. We had never been to this church and really didn't know how things would go. To add more drama to the situation, Monday was a bank holiday and no matter what we were blessed with on Sunday, we wouldn't have access to those funds till Tuesday. My kids saw one of those trampoline parks and said, "Dad, can we go jump?" I mean when you have 3 kiddos ages 13, 10 and 5 in the car day after day in hotels and church meetings, they were awesome, but they also were ready to let go of some energy.

I said, "Well, guys, I would love to go jump. Our funds are low but God is great and He is our provider." Then we claimed the scriptures in Mark 11:22-25:

22And Jesus answering saith unto them, Have faith in God.

23For verily I say unto you, That whosoever shall say unto this mountain, Be thou removed, and be thou cast into the sea; and shall not doubt in his heart, but shall believe that those things which he saith shall come to pass; he shall have whatsoever he saith.

24Therefore I say unto you, What things soever ye desire, when ye pray, believe that ye receive them, and ye shall have them.

25And when ye stand praying, forgive, if ye have ought against any: that your Father also which is in heaven may forgive you your trespasses.

If you look at this passage of scripture it says SAITH three times and BELIEVE once. Being literal here, it means we gotta meditate which means continually rehearse the promise. Our favorite portion of that scripture says, "Whatsoever things you desire, when you pray, believe you receive and you shall have it." Well, I told the kids we gotta have a faith goal—something to believe God for while using these scriptures to put fuel to the fire.

I said, "Let's ask God for $500.00 cash. We don't need a check. This is Saturday as we got into the lovely hotel the church provided. The banks are closed Monday and Cash is best till we get the additional funds from the upcoming meeting." We all prayed in our hotel and believed God.

From that time on, we simply began to thank God for His blessing and His provision. Well, Pastor Jim Brannon called and he and his wife, Janet, desired to take us to a great steakhouse for dinner. Well, that sounded great. Now remember, we had never met them. They were having us because of the recommendation of Jimmy and Becky Pearce.

We sat down in the restaurant with them and the place was beautiful and we all started to look at the menu. Now Pastor Janet is a very talented singer and piano player. But she is also very funny and charismatic. We loved her and Jim quickly. They were grandparents and immediately went into that role to our kids. WELLLLLL. We are looking at what we might order from the menu when suddenly Pastor Janet SAYS in a LOUD VOICE!!! "I almost forgot and I hope this doesn't offend you..."

My heart skipped a beat and I said, "Try me."

"Well, we were on the way over here and I told Jim I have an overwhelming desire to stop by the ATM and get out $500.00 in cash and give it to the Gidley's."

My wife and children all looked at me and it was just like those funny commercials of WHAAAAAASAP!!! Glory to God! We had just prayed a few hours before and she handed $100.00 dollars to each member of my family.

Then she said, "This isn't your offering. This is just what God put on our hearts to give you. Plus if it's ok after dinner, I bet these kids would like to get some energy out. Let's go to the TRAMPOLINE PARK!!!"

Double Blessing!!

Isn't God amazing to answer our prayers and to respond to that scripture passage? Confess with our mouth and believe it in our hearts. As it says in scripture, IT CAME TO PASS!

1 KINGS 17:3

Get thee hence, and turn thee eastward, and hide thyself by the brook Cherith, that is before Jordan.

CHAPTER 10

Heading to the Brook

We love to talk about seasons. There is a purpose and season for everything under the sun. What may looks good to us sometimes (and I find every time) has little to do with the way our Heavenly Father feels about things or how He looks at things. We only know that in the midst of whatever season is upon us that according to His word, He will never ever leave us or forsake us. So the first thing we must get into our heads, and really into our hearts, is that the way we feel about something doesn't mean much.

Take for instance flying in a plane. The first thing a pilot must know is how to read the instruments. Because there are times when you get up there and you cannot see clearly. Things aren't as they appear.

I have heard stories of pilots thinking they were going up when really they were in a nose dive. Others thought they were flying straight while they were heading toward their death all the while just as happy as could be because everything felt good.

Sometimes it's the same way in our Christian life. We must learn to not go by either feeling great or feeling bad. Sometimes our emotions are useless except to gauge where we are in Faith. If we are worried or feeling anxious or if we find ourselves in fear, those things are meant to be a little "check engine" light that comes on in one's spirit to let us know that we are not resting in His hands. There's no reason to go into condemnation over feelings and emotions. A pilot doesn't fly by feelings alone because flying a plane requires **course correction** - checking the instruments is a constant discipline.

Fly By the Instruments

The Holy Spirit is a helper. I ask the Holy Spirit to constantly help me be on **course correction**. Learning to read your instruments in your walk with God is a must to be a champion. Your instrument is the Word of God, the Bible. If you hide the Word in your heart, you will not sin against God. Emotions will try to lead you. The enemy loves somebody that is filled with misguided emotions. Now don't get me wrong, I love it when things are great and we are having a wonderful day and there is plenty of plenty and no sickness and you know the drill. Nothing is challenging you. But we can't trust in that anymore than we can trust when we're down or blue. I have had similar days and felt completely different. It comes down to knowing what the Word of God says. Concerning our thought life Paul addressed this in his letter to the Philippians.

> *8Finally, brethren, whatever is true, whatever is honorable, whatever is right, whatever is pure, whatever is lovely, whatever is of good repute, if there is any excellence and if anything worthy of praise, dwell on these things. 9The things you have learned and received and heard and seen in me, practice these things, and the God of peace will be with you.*

Think on these things. If you're feeling like God isn't near, you must know His Word says that He will never leave you nor forsake you.

Believe me, on this trip, this walk of faith, I had to leave emotions at the door. They were different everyday. We left the house on the 9th of April in 2018. We traveled consistently all over the country ministering April, May, June, July, and August. Now folks, this was a miracle. My wife and I and our three children in a van preaching and singing for five straight months. No home but hotels and no kitchen just restaurants.

Now I must celebrate my wife here because most every woman yearns for her own home and her own kitchen. Her desire is to feed her children correctly and nurture and love her family in a consistent and safe environment. Well, we didn't have that anymore. My wife died to her instincts and followed the word of the Lord for our family. Faith helped her overcome her instincts. Many women would say there is nothing wrong with having a home and a place for my family, in fact, God blessed me with these things. Well folks, sometimes God has other plans to get you somewhere you haven't been and it would be easy to simply say, "This isn't God because isn't a home a good thing to have, isn't security a good thing?"

It's all timing. Everything must be laid at the foot of the Cross. Sabrina was amazing! Our life became hotels and restaurant food. Prior to leaving Aiken, Sabrina and I discussed dietary issues. In the past, our children have had a slight gluten sensitivity. A little trip to a restaurant could possibly set off a reaction. Nothing violent or life threatening but bothersome. Well, we knew the Word of the Lord and we both laid that at the foot of the Cross knowing that the Lord would take care of our diet. Well, I gotta tell you in over five straight months, our children could basically eat anything and not have an adverse reaction. We were constantly in hotels and packing and unpacking. It took an amazing grace, no doubt. But God showed His power to keep us in this journey. Well, as I have said, we were going hard for five months. However, I started to look at our schedule about a month ahead and noticed that it was slowing down. God supernaturally put a schedule together for us. I couldn't take much credit. It was amazing. But I could sense that God was going to be doing something different soon.

I now can see that those months of April-August of 2018 were plowing up the fallow ground in my heart and Sabrina's heart. God did something in us that was cataclysmic. He was breaking up the man-made "foundations of the deep" in our lives with the powerful geyser of His presence which was springing up and shaking everything that we had ever known. It was more than I can describe. You would have to experience it. But when He plows up something, it is because He is going to put some seed there. He is going to make something lovely and amazing. Once in a while, He moves a big tree stump out which requires dynamite. I guess I had a few stumps that had to be taken out. Something was changing and God was getting ready to make a way and show us amazing provision and love.

August 5th 2018. We were at Bethel in Riverside, California. It was pastored at that time by Ron Halvorson. We had a tremendous meeting and God was good. We had lunch and then on the way home to the hotel where Bethel had arranged our stay, I got a text from a man named Rick McMeans. He and his wife Debbie had been members of Bethel for a long time. They were very successful business owners and supporters of their church and the Bethel Christian School, another ministry of Bethel. I knew the McMeans a bit. We had lunch together as a part of a larger group but not intimately as friends. His text said, "Call me when you get to the hotel."

I had Sabrina text him back that I would. I was curious and after we got settled, I called Rick and said, "Hello, Sir, what's up?"

He said, "Tim, Debbie and I are going to be leaving our home in late August and not returning until mid October. We feel the Lord has put something on our hearts."

I said, "What is that?" Well, we don't know where you are planning to go now that the meetings in Riverside are complete."

As Rick was speaking I was thinking in my heart, "Well, that makes two of us." I really didn't know where the Lord was going to put us. As I said the schedule had begun to slow down. One day while in prayer, I had a vision. Traveling as much as I do I have sat on hundreds of planes and sometimes right over the wing. I've noticed when the plane is coming in for a landing that the flaps come out and expand. I had that vision in my mind's eye. I could see that flaps were extending and I knew that meant that after 5 months of straight travel we were coming in for a landing. Now this is California, it's not the easiest place to come in for a landing. It's expensive and well it's expensive LOL! I listened to Rick as he continued.

"While we are gone on our trip, we would love for you to have our house to enjoy and rest and stay in."

On the inside, I was like WOW!!! I said, "Well, let me talk with Jesus and Sabrina."

He said, "No pressure and if it doesn't fit into your plans, no problem."

I called Pastor Ron Halvorson. I told him what Rick said. He said, "How 'bout you take my house and I'll stay at Rick and Debbie's?" We laughed and he said, "Tim, that is a provision from the Lord. They have never done that before and they have been in my church for 32 years."

Now I looked at our schedule and we had meetings up until August 19th and we were to be in Phoenix, AZ. After that I didn't know where we were supposed to go. I didn't have any feeling. I didn't have a tingle. The family was wondering what was next and so was I. But I said to the family, "Guys, I wasn't sure in my flesh if we would last a week after we left South Carolina back in April. God has provided every step of the way. Let's keep praising Him and giving Him glory for what He has done and believe Him for the rest. Our God doesn't know how to fail. He is ever constant and ever true. I'm telling you, I am about to burst forth in the ole song GREAT IS THY FAITHFULNESS. Guys, He is amazing and constant. No bad hair days. He loves us and gave Himself for us. How amazing!!!"

The timing of God is amazing! Wouldn't you know our meetings in Phoenix were to end on August the 19th. Rick called and said, "We are leaving our home on the 18th of August." Just a day later, we arrived after our 6 hour trip from Phoenix to this amazingly beautiful home. I'm thinking 3,000 or so square feet and 4 amazingly decorated bedrooms, a grand staircase, a backyard that overlooked all of Riverside with an outdoor kitchen. Places to Pray and Places to Play! Oh my, I was weeping with gratitude. The devil said, "You have made it up till now, but you're gonna crash and burn." Well, I tell ya, God had another idea - how about a palace in California?! My three children each got their own room. The McMeans had one room that was decorated for their granddaughter who was the same age as our Gracie Bell. Toys and dolls and a beautiful place to rest. Well after five months in a van and hotel rooms and church meetings, we just exploded into that house. No longer in a small hotel room but over 3,000 square feet. I don't think I saw my kids for two days LOL! Now Sabrina's and my room was the Master and, WOW, it had a balcony and I could go on and on. God gave us a palace in Riverside, CA and the McMeans just desired to bless our ministry and be a part of what God was doing. Folks, this is just the beginning of what God was doing in Riverside, CA. After we unpacked a bit and got our kids put away to bed, Sabrina went to sleep and I found myself sitting in the Living Room with this enormous TV. It was 2AM as I sat down. Exhausted and thrilled, I turned on the TV and they had the NFL network. I gushed, "This is of God!!" LOL! I knew my son would be thrilled.

Now the couple of weeks leading up to having the house, the Lord kept letting me know that this provision was similar to the brook Cherith was to Elijah. He blessed us to rest. He required for us to be stationary and, like I said, the previous five months had been a season of plowing up. It was time for the learning and the seed. Like the Brook for the Prophet Elijah, the birds came and fed him. We found the same thing. Supernatural provision. Daily we would hear the flap, flap, flap of the birds. There would be checks in the mail. People who knew we were in the area were blessing us or helping us. We were being taken to breakfast, lunch and dinner. We were being loved on. Remember, people who minister on the road can get very lonely. Take time to love on them. Help them. Bless them. Because many do not. In the next chapter, I will tell you about how this home was not only a resting place but became a Holy Ghost University. God was teaching us. But, back now to our first night there.

I said, "Lord, look what you have done and what you have provided for us. You are amazing!! What do you want me to do?"

The Lord spoke to me and said, "Nothing. I want you to enjoy the next couple weeks and rest. Be with your family."

I smiled and said, "You got it, Lord." I was ready to celebrate and look back at what God had done for our family these past five blessed months. So that's what we did.

Luke 6:38

Give, and it shall be given unto you; good measure, pressed down, and shaken together, and running over, shall men give into your bosom. For with the same measure that ye mete withal it shall be measured to you again.

CHAPTER 11

Gidley Kids Go to Bethel

After being on the road for over five months living by absolute faith, not knowing where we would be sleeping most of the time, ministering in different churches and wherever the Lord opened up the door, we found ourselves in Riverside, CA, in a beautiful home that was given to us for the next few months. One thing we could obviously see was that God was having us reside in Riverside, CA.

I see that name Riverside and it reminds me that He will lead me beside the still waters. Now funny enough, Riverside is a dry river bed. But it was a lovely place for us. We were now in a place where we knew a few people that loved and supported our ministry. We had a place to live. We didn't realize that the Lord was taking us into a more normal existence. The church that was our main contact in that area was Bethel Christian Center pastored by Ron Halvorson. That is where Rick and Debbie McMeans also went to church. They were the folks who had given us the use of their home.

We had so many people there that we loved and our meetings there had been spectacular. Bethel always had so much expectation for what the Lord would do. It was always a joy to preach there and see God touch people. Bethel had (and still has) a Christian school. So here comes the unexpected provision of God. It was a provision that I was not looking for, yet the Father is there providing before we realized that we needed this specific provision in our life. The Word of Faith movement isn't really a movement - it's a lifestyle. However, we are a people that decrees and declares and speaks out by faith what we desire to see happen. Calling those things that are not as though they were. But sometimes and many times we don't know what we need and we need a Father to guide us.

Oh how He loves us and I do believe He loves to surprise us and bless us beyond what we can see! My wife, Sabrina, has always homeschooled and we love it. It has always been something to keep our family together in the midst of traveling. We have amazing kids and God has been good.

Sabrina thought it would be fun for the kids, since we were going to be in this location for a few months, to try out the Christian school at Bethel. Just for a change. I sent a text off to Dr. Mike Crites who had been the principal for many years and now was working more as the overseer. He invited our family in to talk about things. We also talked with the current principal, Mike Pangkee.

We thought we would just have the kids come in for an hour or so and enjoy the socialization. However, they were so kind to us. They said that they would love to host our children during the duration of our time in Riverside and have them come in and enjoy a full schedule. They even said that it would be a blessing to our family. That meant they were blessing all three of our children with free tuition. That meant uniforms and a Chromebook for Maximus so that he could do his studies. Also, Bethel was starting a flag football team and Max was excited to be a part of that also. Giselle and Gracie would also participate in dance class and a few productions. We were completely welcomed and blessed. Dance shoes and costumes were provided for the girls. We were amazed that this school would be so kind and bless our family like this, but again it was scripture coming to life in our life.

Luke 6:38 – "Give, and it shall be given unto you; good measure, pressed down, and shaken together, and running over, shall men give into your bosom."

To be absolutely clear, we never asked for these things. I have seen people abuse their position before and casually mention a need hoping someone would "get the hint." We refused to do that in any way. If God was truly behind and commissioning what we were doing, then providing is HIS problem not mine. Mine is to obey what He says to do and leave the provision to Him. He is our employer and He is good.

So now we are in Riverside, CA, and we are blessed with an amazing home and furthermore we were blessed with something that we had never had which was a spirit-filled school where our children would attend with everything provided. We felt blessed and the kids were excited to do and to be a part of the school. I asked Principal Pangkee if there was anything that I could do to be a blessing back to the school and ministry.

He asked, "How about you come in and do a few chapels during spirit week?"

I was like, "Sure, no problem." We scheduled those chapels.

Unbeknownst to us, a few months prior, the Lord woke Dr. Halvorson early in the morning and had brought our family to mind. Dr. Halvorson is the man who ordained us years ago and since then, we have always looked to him for wisdom and guidance for many years. Following the leading of the Lord, he wrote us a note. The note was a list of things that the Lord gave him to give to us. It was wonderful. It included some slight directions and wisdom for our journey, the strongest message was specifically about Maximus.

One of the things he said was that Maximus, our oldest who was 13 at this time, ought to be in a spirit-filled school and that Max was really our priority at this time. Our girls were still very young and were fine, but he felt Maximus should be in a school. Well this was a challenge when we first heard it because we were on this faith journey and traveling and how in the world would we travel full-time and have Maximus in a school. It was one of those times that we were a bit confused about how to bring that about and be faithful to the word. But faith is the victory that overcomes the world and we simply said, "Lord, we want to obey and do what you want. Show us the way and we will follow."

So about three months later we found ourselves in Riverside, CA, with a home provided and now a school provided not just for Maximus but our dear girls also. God brought the word to pass. Max and the girls flourished in this situation and were a blessing. The staff told us that they were just blessed to have our children in their school. The staff loved them and said that they were a blessing to the school body.

Well, we did the Chapel services. The Holy Spirit moved in such a powerful way. We had 25 kids give their hearts to Jesus during the first service. It was an amazing atmosphere of the Spirit of God and then we had the Friday chapel a couple days later. We had an altar service and had over 100 kids at the altar. I was laying hands on big guys and would feel the hot tears on my hands as we would pray. Kids would have the power of God on them and just fall down in joy and elation. Now here is the thing: many of these kids didn't know about the power of God or what was going on. Many of these kids didn't come from Christian homes. Bethel had opened their school up to many that had had problems in their former public schools and were being given a second chance in this environment. Kids were blitzed under this amazing move of God. They would ask us, "What is this that I'm feeling? Why am I on the floor? What happened?" LOL!

This was fun because I simply told them, "This is your Creator telling you that He loves you and wants to help and bless you." Well, this led to laughter and Joy. Kids who didn't really know if anyone really cared for them started to have prayer requests for grandparents and siblings and other family issues. I had one teacher that had been with the school for over two decades say, "We have never had a move of God like this. This is amazing. Can we go on?"

Kids were asking for each other's forgiveness and making things right with each other. That is how you know revival is near; when people begin to make things right. It's real repentance. Now I could see why God made it possible for our children to go to that school. One of the reasons was because He purposed to bring a move of God. He showed that the kids could encounter the power of God even without knowing what it means to be slain in the Spirit. There is a hole on the inside of us that is only meant for Christ to fill. We try other things, people, money, whatever. As the song "Calvary's Love" says,

Only Jesus, Only He

Brings redemption, full and free

There's a yearning, in all our lives

That only Jesus SATISFIES.

Romans 12:3

For I say, through the grace given unto me, to every man that is among you, not to think of himself more highly than he ought to think; but to think soberly, according as God hath dealt to every man the measure of faith.

CHAPTER 12

Going Deeper

Sabrina and I found ourselves in a new world. During my former schedule, Sabrina had been a "single mother." Many don't understand the life of someone who is itinerant and speaks or sings on the road.

In fact, what most people don't realize, especially those in itinerant ministry, is the hidden hazards involved in this type of ministry. It's like carrying a bucket of fire through a dry forest. If you make a mistake, you risk burning the whole thing down! Fire is good and powerful in the right place, and the most important fire to keep lit is the one at home.

In the beginning of our ministry, I would drive everywhere. God gave us a very beautiful van. We didn't have any children and Sabrina and I have always been very much in love as well as best friends. It was amazing to do what we were good at and called to do. But, as you know, when children arrive, things change. You try and say that things won't change but they do. Sabrina has been an amazing partner in this ministry and I missed her so much after Maximus was born. We tried to continue to travel the way that we had in the past and I was very stubborn not preferring things to change. I put undue pressure on my wife to continue to travel with me because people loved it when she would dance ballet while I would sing.

God always brings about change so that we might grow into His image. Sabrina was patient with me, but I soon realized that she couldn't be with me all the time and raise our son in the best way. So, I began to travel on the weekends - flying out on Friday or Saturday morning and returning Sunday night or Monday. Then I would have a few days at home to be in the office, so that I could be on the phone and keep the ministry going. Calling Pastors and booking meetings is the name of the game. You have to be called to do it but you also have to be ready to graduate from it.

Once we calculated how much I was gone in a year. It would be six months away and obviously [for our math majors] that is six months at home. How many of you desire to miss six months of your child's first year. I mean, really? Sabrina would travel when possible or when it was within driving distance but we purposed for her to be at home and enjoy the consistency.

For years this was our system for most of the time. I'm sure I went too long that way and I'm sure God had other plans. But many times we get hooked in and hunker down into what we are doing without really looking and watching in prayer for what we should do. (I really didn't plan on revealing this in this book!) I encourage those who travel for work or ministry. My sober advice is to not sacrifice your family or children for the sake of the Gospel. There are many people called to care for the body of Christ. But only one is called to look after the affairs of your family. THAT IS YOU! Especially when the children grow beyond five years old, they desperately require their father. God knows this and He will help you by giving you wisdom in the transition.

The year before we went on this adventure of faith I was gone three different times in the year for almost three weeks. It was three weeks hearing my children's voices by phone or looking at my wife through the screen of a computer or phone. I simply could not and would not do it anymore that way. In 2018 it was marvelous because we launched out as a family and we were together for 50 outta the 52 weeks of that year. The other weeks were when Sabrina and I were in Israel and our kids stayed in California with Evan and Shanna Perez and their kiddos. It was amazing always being together and being able to be a real "hands-on-he's-all-here" dad. Granted, we were on the road, but we were together.

Now back to the story. God provides this school and our children are gone from 8 a.m. to 3 p.m. everyday. Sabrina and I dropped them at school the first time and we looked at each other and thought, "What do we do now?" We had always homeschooled them for their entire lives. Now we were free to do other things. Sabrina and I rediscovered one another during that time and we also found that God had taken us to Riverside and had brought about these circumstances for us to go deeper in Him. Leaving everything and being on the road and traveling from church to church, ministry to ministry, faith to faith, glory to glory had done something in our entire family. **It had broken up the fallow ground.** The vast change, going off in the direction called faith, had broken up the ground in our hearts and minds. So now with our children in school and our days to ourselves, we found that God had placed us in Riverside, CA, to read and learn and wait upon Him in prayer. The ground of our hearts were now ready to receive the seeds that He desired to plant.

He desired to and did change our lives.

We learned many lessons. One of the beauties of staying at Rick and Debbie's house was the amazing amount of excellent books available to read. However, it seemed that the Lord was drawing us to Andrew Wommack's books. We read many different ones. It caused us to see many things in the light of the Word. Many things I had felt the Lord showing me, but they were right there in front of me in black and white. I can remember being so excited about what we were being shown. The first five months of the trip had caused such a major shift. Because we were pulled away from the "more normal" routine, I could see that God was shaking my reality to be able to show me something and to embed it in my heart. We were receiving at a very deep and profound level. Things were clear and it was affecting our ministry.

In Andrew Wommack's book, A Better Way to Pray I was seeing something so crystal clear and God allowed this message to really plant into my heart. What was it? Well, something that most in Christianity would call a "cleeshay" (or for the learned folk, *cliché*): **the authority of the believer**. I was seeing that most of the time we are asking God for things that He has already said yes to or that His Word has already bestowed upon us. It occurred to me that it was an unbelieving prayer to ask God for healing. Allow me to explain.

According to the Word of God, we see that God looks at things in the past tense because He is outside of time. For instance, Ephesians 1:3 - "Blessed be the God and Father of our Lord Jesus Christ who HATH blessed us with ALL spiritual blessings in Christ Jesus." Without going too deep, all spiritual blessings means everything that we require has already been given and bestowed upon us to accomplish what ought to be done in this world.

We already have it. When we ask the Lord for something that we already have, we are going against His Word. He grants us authority to rule and reign. In Acts 3, it says Peter and John when they were at the gate called Beautiful said to the crippled man, "Silver and gold have I none. BUT SUCH AS I HAVE, I give you in the name of Jesus of Nazareth." Did you see it - **SUCH AS I HAVE?** Peter said in his writings in

> *2 Peter 1:1 - "Simon Peter, a servant and an apostle of Jesus Christ, to them that have obtained LIKE PRECIOUS FAITH with us through the righteousness of God and Savior Jesus Christ."*

Galatians 2:20 says, "I am crucified with Christ; nevertheless I live; yet not I but Christ liveth in me; and the life which I now live in the flesh I live BY THE FAITH OF THE SON OF GOD, who loved me and gave Himself for me."

We see in the Word of God that our faith that we have is the same faith that Peter and Paul had. It is not correct to say, "Oh I wish I had the faith of Peter." We DO! Because you got yours from the Same Source where He got His; from the Son of God. Peter said to the Crippled Man, "For such as I have." This is something that we carry on the inside of us.

We are all given according to Romans 12:3:

"For I say, through the grace given unto me, to every man that is among you, not to think of himself more highly than he ought to think; but to think soberly, according as God hath dealt to every man the measure of faith."

The measure of Faith is not based on a measure of our making or miniscule understanding. It's the same measure from the same source — THE MEASURE from Christ Himself.

Some reading this may have heard the story of the visitation that Kenneth Hagen had from Jesus. While Jesus was teaching him a few things, a demon showed up and started to distract Brother

Hagen. Jesus kept on speaking as if the demon wasn't present. Bro. Hagen kept waiting for Jesus to deal with this thing and Jesus wasn't doing anything. Finally, being frustrated and upset Bro. Hagen said, "Excuse me, Lord" and looked at the demon and said, "In His name, Jesus, get out of here right now!" The demon scampered away. Then Bro. Hagen said to Jesus, "Lord, why wouldn't you rebuke that demon."

Jesus said, "Son, I have already done everything that I'm ever gonna do about the enemy." Suddenly Bro. Hagen understood that Jesus had already given us authority over all the power of the enemy. WOW! My heart was rejoicing at this revelation!

Brother Wommack spoke of times of healing ministry where they don't ask the Lord to do what He has already done. He speaks directly to the body or body part or what the issue may be and in the name of Jesus addresses the thing by name. Well, this changed my ministry and we began to see the Mighty Hand of God that He had put upon us. It was the **authority** to speak to things. To pray the prayer of faith as James says. It isn't a begging prayer; it is speaking directly to the illness name and telling the thing to go in Jesus' name. We have seen wonderful things happen.

One time I was getting ready to fly from California to do some meetings in the Dallas area. We were about 10 minutes out from leaving the house in Riverside to go to the airport when I heard my youngest daughter crying. She had turned her foot and injured it. The front on the house had some beautiful travertine stone. She had injured her foot there. Sabrina came upstairs quickly with a look of great concern. She said, "Tim, the top of Gracie's foot is turning black and blue. I think she broke it!"

Grace couldn't put any weight on the foot. So we sat her down to rest on the bed. I began to examine the foot and yep, it didn't look too good. Black and blue and even felt that a bone was outta place. Apart from my concern for my sweet Gracie, my first thought was, "Here I am ready to go minister and this happens." Then suddenly the Lord reminded me of what I had been studying and the Lord challenged me to speak directly to the foot. He assured me, "You already know that by My stripes, she was healed, past tense. You know that I have already provided for this before Grace was born."

1 Peter 2:24 and Isaiah 53:5 BY WHOSE STRIPES YOU WERE HEALED. You don't have to ask for what has already been given!

I took my little girl's foot in my hand and I said, "Lord, I thank you for the stripes on Your back and by the authority of the Word of God, Gracie is already healed." Then I spoke directly to the foot. I was specific. I said, "Gracie's right foot. I command you to be healed of this injury now in the name of Jesus. Bone, if you are indeed broken, you are now healed. Ligaments, if you are torn, you are now repaired." I tell you I saw black and blue retreat and I saw swelling disappear before my very eyes. I saw a lovely pinkish hue come into that foot and then I said, "Grace put your weight on it."

She was so brave. She slowly put her foot down and I will never forget the look on her face when she had no pain. We rejoiced! The foot heard me and was healed. Such as Daddy had, I gave to Grace. We then got in the car and the family took me to the airport. I felt like I could have flown to Dallas all by myself without an airplane! What a Savior we have!

Acts 8:26-27

And the angel of the Lord spake unto Philip, saying, Arise, and go toward the south unto the way that goeth down from Jerusalem unto Gaza, which is desert. And he arose and went: and, behold, a man of Ethiopia, an eunuch of great authority under Candace queen of the Ethiopians, who had the charge of all her treasure, and had come to Jerusalem for to worship,...

CHAPTER 13

A Holy Ghost Introduction

A few weeks after moving to Riverside, CA, I had done a concert out of state and was flying back to California from a ministry date and upon landing was going to sing at a conference for Jim Wiloughby. He had invited me because he desired for other pastors in the area to be exposed to our ministry.

I'll pause here to say thank you to Randy and Ginger Bumgardner for picking me up at the airport and getting me to the church. Traffic can be a challenge in Souther California and they have lived there for many years. So thank you!

I sang that night and God was good to us. We had great fellowship and the night was especially wonderful because the keynote speaker was Bishop James Owens. He and his lovely wife, Lynette, were on fire for God and he spoke a "now" word to the body that night. The altar service was amazing. Afterwards, we met briefly. He and his wife loved my voice and offered to have us join them for a meal.

We quickly followed up with one another and scheduled a time to have lunch. We had wonderful fellowship. They told me they were getting ready for an outdoor event in Hemet, CA. They asked if I would be available to sing for the event. I gladly accepted the invitation and then they said, "We would also like you to come and have dinner with us and meet the rest of our ministry team and the others that will be ministering throughout the event."

The event was not a long distance from our temporary home there in Riverside. We went up the mountain and the views of Riverside were captivating. It seemed like the moon itself could have been picked off the branch like an apple. I could sense in my spirit that the Lord desired for us at the event and to meet these people. It was great to have the opportunity to meet other people that loved the Lord and were in this same location in Southern California.

We walked into a lovely home which belonged to someone on Bishop Owens' ministry team. It was a large place and we met several other ministers along with their wives. Dinner was being prepared. Bishop Owens asked everyone to come into the large living area. He indicated that each person should introduce themselves and their ministry. Well, the way we were seated, Sabrina and I were the last ones to say anything and you've gotta remember that we didn't know anyone at the meeting except for Bishop Owens and his wife, Lynette. People would stand and say their name and where they were from and a brief ministry synopsis. It was very nice.

Then they came to the end. I remember there were close to 25 people in the room. Given that we were all in the ministry, there wasn't anyone present that was shy. So by the time they got to Sabrina and me, it had been 15 minutes or so of introductions. As I stood to my feet, my full intention was to say "Hello" and state our names. However, God had something different that totally changed the atmosphere.

I said, "Hello, my name is Tim Gidley and my wonderful wife, Sabrina. The ministry's name is Crown Voice Ministries." The atmosphere changed and — my God I can feel it now as I write this — there were people crying, groaning in the spirit, springing forth like a waterfall. It was like I missed something that had been going on. It was like a time warp on the Starship Anointing because we had barely started and somehow we skipped to the end. Surely this is what we would normally experience at the end of a mighty sermon which called for the consecration of the body present. But no, I simply introduced ourselves. Bishop James was under the power of God. He stumbled toward me and I laid hands on him. He went out under the power of the Spirit of God. Lynette, his wife, and Bishop James' mother came forward and I laid hands on them and the power of God hit them. Soon we were prophesying and speaking words of knowledge over all these different ministries from all over California. I can't help but tell you it was like an altar service that simply exploded forth outta nowhere.

My words were normal. But God hit that place. People were on the ground weeping before the Lord. We had a few people that were healed. The fire of God touched people. The prophetic words and "words of knowledge" the Lord gave us were very specific as we were told instructions and answers to prayer for the people represented. The evening resulted in several invitations to speak and minister. Some were television and internet ministries. Some were churches and precious congregations.

I've never experienced anything like it before. God just showed up and blessed His people and it was a blessing for us also. It continued to build our faith and let us know we were right where God desired for us to be.

But God didn't just give us connections through ministry meetings. He would connect us with hungry hearts right on the streets. He knows where to send you and how to use you. Our family was excited to embrace the connections that God had in mind for us. For our next part of the journey, God sent us up to San Francisco.

Go to Korea

Just as we were on our way to San Francisco, the Lord spoke to me and said, "I'm going to send you to Korea." How was that possible when it was clear that we were supposed to be going to San Francisco? In San Francisco, we were visiting a family there for a few days before we went over to Paradise, CA, to minister. We suddenly just desired to take a walk and enjoy the cool sweatshirt weather for which San Francisco is noted. We walked up the street heading toward the park. We saw a Korean Church that was having a yard sale. We went over and shopped around a bit. Then my wife got into a conversation with one of the members of the church. My wife told them a little about our ministry and that I was a singer. Well, that was it. The Korean lady said, "YOU SING?"

I said, "YES!"

She said, "YOU SING, YOU SING NOW."

LOL!

Well, I just took off into "Amazing Grace" and this yard sale began to be an instant meeting of believers. A man came up to me and his name was Samuel Lee. We talked for a minute. Then I said, "Raise your hands, brother." He did and my whole family laid hands on that humble man of God.

We went to eat. I didn't think that when I came to San Francisco I would be sitting down with a Korean pastor. But, now the word that the Lord had given me made complete sense! Here I was sitting with a pastor from Korea and his brother pastors a huge church in Korea. He told me he desired the Holy Ghost and that his church needed the Holy Ghost too. He asked us to come and minister at the church. I was the first non-Korean minister to minister in that church in it's 50 year history. We sang and laid hands on people. It was a thrilling time.

It all came from simply desiring to take a walk. I thought I just fancied some fresh air and it turned out there was a Korean church that needed some encouragement. I also got a real nice tie from the garage sale. :-)

Ask the Lord to use you. Be ready in season and out of season. Ask Him. I dare you. He will use you in ways you couldn't even imagine. These are just a couple of stories from our time in California. But I have much more to tell you. Turn the page...

I KINGS 17:24

And the woman said to Elijah, Now by this I know that thou art a man of God, and that the word of the Lord in thy mouth is truth.

CHAPTER 14

Brook of Cherith to the Widow of Zeraphath

After you have taken an unimaginable step of faith, God invites you to the next step of faith. Remember when we were coming to the end of the first part of our trip? We had been on the road for five months and 10 days. It was on August 5th that we received the invitation to take Rick and Debbie's home while they were on their RV trip. It was during those last couple weeks of meetings in Arizona when the Lord showed me that being at Rick and Debbie's house would be like Elijah being beside the brook Cherith from 1 Kings 17.

> *¹And Elijah the Tishbite, who was of the inhabitants of Gilead, said unto Ahab, As the Lord God of Israel liveth, before whom I stand, there shall not be dew nor rain these years, but according to my word. ²And the word of the Lord came unto him, saying, ³Get thee hence,*

*and turn thee eastward, and hide thyself by
the brook Cherith, that is before Jordan. ⁴And it
shall be, that thou shalt drink of the brook; and
I have commanded the ravens to feed thee there.
⁵So he went and did according unto the word
of the Lord: for he went and dwelt by the brook
Cherith, that is before Jordan. ⁶And the ravens
brought him bread and flesh in the morning,
and bread and flesh in the evening; and he
drank of the brook.*

What the Lord was showing me, and I believe
also warning me, was that our fast-paced
ministry time since leaving our home on April
9th of 2018 and constantly traveling was going
to stop. He did with us as He did with his Old
Testament prophet, Elijah. He was going to set us
in a place and have us rest and that "the Ravens"
would supply us.

That is exactly what happened. We got there
and crashed for a bit. I explained how God took
our kids to Bethel Christian Academy which gave
Sabrina and me abundant time to study and pray.
God enrolled us in school too. God opened doors.
But compared to the past, we didn't minister as
much during this time. God brought the Ravens.
People would mail us gifts and checks outta
nowhere with notes that said, "Just thinking of
you," "Wanting to be a blessing to you," or "Thank

you for your ministry." It was a refreshing and humbling time. To this day, people that started to partner with our ministry during those days are still partners now. Indeed, God joins people to you.

It's in my spirit to tell you that during this time we had changed the name of our ministry from Tim Gidley Ministries Inc. to CROWN VOICE MINISTRIES INC. Why? I began to be uncomfortable with seeing my name. I began to not care what people said about us or what opinions were of other people. I just wanted to serve God and get His Word out to the people, the true meat of the Word. I then had a dream where I saw a large beautiful restaurant. The name of the place was CROWN CUTS. I walked in and smelled the most amazing steak I had ever smelled. It was like a Texas De Brazil. Meat of every kind. I saw someone in a chef's uniform cutting these lovely sides of meat and putting them on people's plates. I went closer and realized that I was the CHEF. I was cutting the meat.

I awoke from this dream and suddenly I could remember Paul saying that the Churches should grow up—get off of the milk and get to the meat of the Word: 1 Corinthians 3:2

I knew that God was getting ready to transition me from being known primarily as a singer to someone that could break open the Word of

Almighty God. I knew the ministry's name was to be CROWN VOICE MINISTRIES. So we went through the process with the IRS and did away with the Tim Gidley Ministries label and opened a new ministry called CROWN VOICE MINISTRIES.

I had met Myles Monroe a few years ago when I was singing for the same conference where he was speaking and we had dinner a few times. For some reason, while there were many other people at our table such as the conference host, Myles would talk with me, the Singer, LOL. He was the one who told me about being a subject instead of a citizen. He said, "Tim, I am from the Bahamas. I grew up with the Queen of England being my Sovereign. What she said went. Every morning, walking to school with my friends, I would stop and put our hands on the feet of the statue of the Queen. However, you in America have citizenship. You have rights, you can disagree with your leadership. But someone that is a subject of the Kingdom is simply there to do their master's bidding."

I thought then, "Why are you telling me this?" I now understand that conversation. CROWN VOICE MINISTRIES is meant to represent the Crown. My voice has always been a musical voice, yet God had been bringing forth the Prophetic Voice over the last few years. God wanted a ministry of not just music but someone who could proclaim prophetically to His people.

Also and most important is that we are to be Ambassadors of this Kingdom, not proclaiming our own name. The headline was no longer "Tim Gidley." Now is the time to be a true Ambassador of this Kingdom which certainly has a King. KING JESUS. I know that we are called Citizens of Heaven. But the Kingdom doesn't have citizens, the Kingdom has subjects. Subjects do the bidding of the King. Our lives are fulfilled as agents of the King who participate with Him to see that His will be done on earth as it is in heaven.

Amazing how God would bring Myles Monroe to Orlando, FL, a few times to help me understand the requirement to lay down my rights as a Citizen and go everyday and lay my hands on the Feet of King Jesus and be a subject.

After being at Rick and Debbie's home for almost 90 days, we required new direction from the Lord if we were to stay in the area. Rick and Debbie were going to come back soon and we were to vacate the house. Well, we received the answers to our prayer that the kids should stay in the school. They were to stay in until the end of the semester and that was still a few months away. So that meant that we were required to find another place. Instantly our flesh gets uncomfortable and we start hearing the enemy say things like, "You had a nice house, but do you know what it costs to live in this area of California?"

I told my wife who was trusting Jesus with me, "Don't tell anybody about this. I don't wanna manipulate anything. God gave us this place and He has another place for us to complete the mission." I began to walk the beautiful backyard of the home that we had and say, "Ya know, Devil, this house has been amazing but the next place is gonna have a pool in it."

LOL. It was hot in SoCal and I just had it in me to say it.

I was not going to be intimidated by the Devil. I have the Faith of the Son of God. He is King Jesus and Jesus takes care of His subjects. The Father in Heaven sent us and He will provide. The Holy Spirit will lead us. Many questions arose at this time. If you rent a house, that is a bit of money with a deposit and the first month's rent, but did we want to commit to a lease for a year?. Places that were by the month weren't very nice and the location wasn't suitable. Our requirement was to be near the school. I would always love taking the kids to school in the morning because we would go down VICTORIA RD. Victory all the way to what God provides.

Time was ticking and nothing was showing up. No provision yet, but I knew the Provider. "YOU'RE GONNA END UP IN A HOTEL!" I would hear the Enemy say.

"NO, I am well provided for, Devil, and the next place has A POOL."

Well, one day, as things were getting to be about 10 days away from moving out to NOWHERE, the Lord reminded me that this place had been like the Brook Cherith. I said, "Yes, Lord, I remember." He said go read the Word and see what happens next.

"Are you serious?"

"Yes," He said. "Go read 1 Kings 17."

"So you want me to go read a story of the prophet Elijah that happened thousands of years ago so that I can know what is going to happen in the next 10 days?"

Then the Lord said, "Yeah, that's it."

So I got my Bible out!!

PROVERBS 3:5-6

Trust in the Lord with all thine heart; and lean not unto thine own understanding. In all thy ways acknowledge him, and he shall direct thy paths.

CHAPTER 15

The Widow of Zeraphath

I told my wife Sabrina what the Lord had said to do. Get your Bible, check out 1 Kings 17, and see what I did with the prophet Elijah. She kinda looked at me with the same tone as I had responded to the Lord. "Are you serious?" LOL!

"Yes! It's what He said to do." So we got the Word and began to read 1 Kings 17.

> *¹And Elijah the Tishbite, who was of the inhabitants of Gilead, said unto Ahab, As the Lord God of Israel liveth, before whom I stand, there shall not be dew nor rain these years, but according to my word. ²And the word of the Lord came unto him, saying, ³Get thee hence, and turn thee eastward, and hide thyself by the brook Cherith, that is before Jordan. ⁴And it shall be, that thou shalt drink of the brook; and I have commanded the ravens to feed thee there.*

*⁵So he went and did according unto the word
of the Lord: for he went and dwelt by the brook
Cherith, that is before Jordan. ⁶And the ravens
brought him bread and flesh in the morning,
and bread and flesh in the evening; and he
drank of the brook.*

We had already experienced 1 Kings 17:3-6. We
had already experienced the wonder of these
verses. Now I read verse number 7:

*⁷And it came to pass after a while, that the
brook dried up, because there had been no rain
in the land.*

Then verse 8!! I love the number 8; it is the
number of new beginnings.

*⁸And the word of the Lord came unto him,
saying, ⁹Arise, get thee to Zarephath, which
belongeth to Zidon, and dwell there: behold, I
have commanded a widow woman there to
sustain thee.*

Well, we don't have a place called Zarephath in
California. But the Lord said "ARISE and Go!!" I
told Sabrina, "Honey, there is a woman that is
supposed to sustain us during this time. I don't
know if she is a widow but I know it's a woman."

Now when the Lord says, "Arise and Go," how do
you do that? BY FAITH! One must have a change

of attitude. It means there's an adjustment of heart and mind. We realize that it's not up to us to figure this thing out. It's up to you or if you're married then both of you must receive it by faith. Have a willingness. The flesh prompts us to stay where we are because it seems like we're settled or comfortable. But, when the Lord said "Arise and go," by His Word, Sabrina and I settled it. We let go of Cherith and began to receive Zeraphath by Faith. Now this was the Word. We settled it and then didn't begin to scheme and find a way. We began to praise the Lord. We gave Him thanks that He had given us a word to claim—a revelation. It was something that we could put our faith toward.

There was one family in Southern California that God had knit into our lives: Evan and Shawnna Perez with their kids, Tatum and Hunter. God was speaking to them and moving in their lives so much. God had already shown His mighty hand of protection over them by nullifying false accusations at work concerning Shawnna's career. They had received amazing provision to pay off the debt from Evan's medical training. They knew the Voice of God. They were in the audience at Bethel when we preached the first time in Riverside. Their daughter, Tatum, had whispered to her momma that she hoped to give a few dresses to my youngest Gabriella. She gave so many things and, just like the Lord would orchestrate, everything fit perfectly. Well, the Perez family was touched by our Word of Faith that we preached that day. They were touched by our commitment to Living by Faith.

Evan left the service and was in the bathroom. (God speaks to me there also, LOL!) However the Lord spoke to him and said, "I brought you a family that is walking by faith so that you could learn how to do it for what I have in store for you." To learn more about the Perez Family testimony, it's available to read in Appendix A.

During this time I believe they were the only ones that knew that we required a place to go and time was running out. They have such a heart for God and His people and a true love for our family. They even prayed and asked the Lord if they were to move outta their home and give it to us for our time in California. WOW! How many people would even put that before the Lord? It is no wonder to me why this family is blessed. We are blessed to know them. But the Lord told them, "No." That is because God had another wonder to perform. He showed that He still can hold a Ram in the thicket for us. He proved that He is still Jehovah Jireh. He is my Provider.

Another thing going on during this time: I was required to go to Florida to be on the CTN flagship show, "THE GOOD LIFE." This coincided with the very weekend that we were to move out of Rick and Debbie McMeans' home. I had a flight that was leaving at 1AM on Monday morning. Rick and Debbie were coming back on Monday around 12 Noon. The enemy was yelling that my family would be in a hotel while I flew to Florida. A quick thank you to dear friends Dr. Andy and Jeri Kartsen for purchasing the ticket to Florida for us. They came outta nowhere to be a blessing at the most perfect time. God puts people in your life to help you accomplish your mission.

My presence was required on THE GOOD LIFE because they were doing a show on a gentlemen that was and is still a dear friend of mine Gus Bess. Gus is an amazing guy. Go to https://amzn.to/2S89Ukt and order his book *If There is a God, Wouldn't You Want to Know Him?* I had known Gus from around 2005 when I sang in a church that he pastored. He had just taken the Church in Tucson, AZ, and they had me on the schedule. He told me later with a laugh that he never liked singers. They never acted very good. LOL. But he loved me and Sabrina. Maximus was just a few months old, I believe. Well, I missed fellowshipping with Gus for years and we reconnected and he was pastoring in California. It had been over 10 years. I came out to sing and minister for Him. While we were together, he would tell me of his life journey and all that God had done. I heard the Lord speak to me and say, "I want you to help him get a book published."

I called a good friend of mine named John Mason. John is a beautiful man - the kind of guy you would desire to be with for hours on end just listening to the wisdom that pours from him. He is an amazing speaker. We met around 2006. He was speaking and I was singing. John was very instrumental in the beginning of John Bevere and his host of great books. I called John regarding Gus. I didn't know how to get a book completed or published but my friend John would know. John and Gus developed a great relationship and, yes, a wonderful book came forth. I also helped Gus by sending his book to my friends, Bob and Jane D'Andrea, the founders of Christian Television Network. They had Gus on the show and asked me to be there to kinda get people familiar with Gus and sing on the show between interview segments.

While all of this was going on and I had about three days until I was supposed to leave and also that we were to leave Rick and Debbie's home to go where? LOL! I didn't know. I told my wife, "There is no way I can get on a plane at 1 AM knowing that y'all have to be out of this house 11 hours later. I should to be here." To go where? I still didn't know.

But Sabrina is a warrior in faith. She said, "You are going to Florida. We minister. That is what we do. We will be fine. If we go to a hotel, then we will go. You will be back in 2 days and we will see what happens." I was like WOW! What a woman of faith! To be willing to give up everything and follow the Lord with all of her heart. Many folks would wilt at the slightest hint of inconvenience, not Sabrina Gidley!

FRIDAY MORNING BEFORE THE FLIGHT!! Three short days till I'm on a plane and my family is... going where? I woke up Friday and I was in between awake and asleep. I heard the Lord say these words, "KEEP YOUR MOUTH RIGHT, STAY IN PRAISE." My spirit within me exploded with expectation. This was the Lord saying, "Listen, I am bringing a miracle to pass so don't mess things up with your mouth."

It would be easy to mess up–to hamper the Spirit with doubt or worry. We were under so much pressure. We didn't know exactly what was going on, but our assignment was to stay in Praise. Calling those things that are not as though they were. Romans 4. Giving God praise for what He had DONE and what He was obviously GOING TO DO. We learn to Dance even before the music starts. We ought to learn to keep dancing when it seems as if the music has stopped. We go by FAITH and, no, it's not blind Faith. Faith doesn't know any handicaps or limitations. It goes by the Word of God. There is a promise in the Word of God for everything we face. Faith grabs the promise and thanks the Lord and praises in the midst of circumstances. If you feel like the Lord has left you, then you have this promise that says, I WILL NEVER LEAVE YOU NOR FORSAKE YOU. If you feel like provision is far and the Lord is going to let you down, then the Word of God says in Philippians 4, "My God SHALL, He Shall, provide all of my needs according to His riches in glory by CHRIST JESUS!"

We had a family meeting on Saturday morning, October 13, 2018. Monday morning was getting closer. I reminded my family of something that Sabrina's Dad says to the kids when they are trying something new and having difficulty. He would say, "COWBOY UP!" meaning grow up, take responsibility, and do your best. Don't whine. The whole family understood and smiled. We reviewed the promises of God and how far God had brought us on this journey. The Bible says that Israel forgot God days without number. I look at all the miracles that God did for Israel and I'm thinking, "How could these people ever doubt God again?!" But when we complain and murmur we do the same thing. I was determined not to go down that path. The family was too. After the meeting, we all went our separate ways. Boxes with our possessions that we had with us on the trip were packed heading for God knows where. I went into the TV room and my son, Maximus, was sitting on the couch. He desperately desired to stay in the area so that he could finish football season and continue at Bethel. He looked up with his eyes a bit teary. "Dad? Where are we going to go?"

I said, "Pal, I don't know. All I know is that God sent us and He has and will provide for us." He smiled and went back to watching football.

I found out later that my wife was upstairs on the floor praying and crying. "Lord, where are we going? What will we do?" It was a difficult time. Many emotions were dangling within all of us to desperately get out and have a flesh exhibition. LOL!

After this I got into the car to go get some milk and a few small items that were required. I was praying and praising to the best of my ability. Praise was my focus because I couldn't be stagnant or start down the road of doubt. I had to keep my mind and faith busy. Because I would begin to try to work things out in my flesh. This was war, not just with the enemy, but with myself. It was an inner battle to control myself and to cultivate the fruit of the Spirit called Self-control.

I was coming back over the bridge of the 91 Interstate and taking the La Sierra Drive exit when the phone rang and it was our friend Andy Kartsen. He is a lovely man, a very successful guy who doesn't just speak to waste words. He was direct. "Hey Buddy, I believe we have found a place for you."

I was astonished, "How did you know?"

He said, "You need to call a lady named Mandy Reed. She goes to Bethel and she has a guest house on her property."

Well, I drove back to the house. I gathered Sabrina. I told Max that Mom and I were going to go out and would be back in an hour. En route, we were on the phone with Mandy and she was so wonderful. She is from Puerto Rico and I just love her accent. She calls her speech "Spanglish." LOL. She said, "Getting to our place is difficult, so I will meet you and guide you in."

How? What happened that this provision was coming to pass? Remember the day before, the Lord said on Friday morning, "KEEP YOUR MOUTH RIGHT AND STAY IN PRAISE!!" Later that day, Mandy was heading to Bethel for a class she was taking at the college. A lady named Julia Thronson that was a part of the Bethel Church staff talked to Mandy and said, "You know Tim Gidley, right?"

Mandy said, "Yes, of course." She had been in our meetings at Bethel. Later I found out that I had a prophetic word and laid hands on Mandy in a previous meeting and she was delivered from a trauma in her earlier life.

Julia said, "Tim and his family are needing a place to go after leaving Rick and Debbie's. Would it be possible for them to stay in your guest cottage for a short while?"

Mandy said, "I have had Tim Gidley's face in front of me for two weeks. I just pray and pray for him and his family. I thought it was just a prayer assignment. But God must have been preparing me for their need."

We followed Mandy out to their place. It was a nice drive of about 20 minutes into the mountains behind Riverside, CA. We turned into this gorgeous equestrian community. Then we made our way to their home. When I saw Mandy I knew exactly who she was and remembered prophesying over her. She welcomed us and took us to meet Dave. We instantly loved Dave; a warmer kinder man you will never meet. Mandy's only condition for us coming would be Dave saying "yes." We walked through their amazing home and then graduated to the back yard.

I could hardly believe my eyes. So many flowers and beauty everywhere. A few months before I had a dream of a property with fruit trees. Well, there it was just as I saw it in my dream. It had the most inviting pool with a rock slide and a jacuzzi. I crooned, "THERE IS THE POOL, DEVIL!" LOL. They showed us the bath house that had a beautiful bathroom and sauna to sit in and sweat. There was a basketball court and beside it was a horseshoe pit. Dave pointed up on top of the hill and said, "That gazebo is great to see sunsets." That place became a great place of prayer and communion with the Lord. I had desired a Pool, yet Sabrina told me that she asked the Lord for a Vista. From that Gazebo you could see a 360° view of snow-covered mountains all the way to BIG BEAR. Sabrina was blessed because she had her VISTA!! We walked to the back of the property and there was this lovely coy pond with turtles. It was an acre or so of lush vegetation and amazing grass area for volleyball or throwing the football. Pathways through the bushes and trees for prayer walks.

One of my favorite things was the gas fire pit. Turn a knob, gas comes on, light a match, and we have made fire. It was wonderful. The cottage was gorgeous and came with a beautiful dog named Molly, a Snow White Lab, and the most loving dog I have ever met. We owe Molly a big debt and I will tell that story later. The cottage was much smaller than what we had at Rick and Debbie's but it was so beautiful and you could step out the door just a few steps from the pool. It had an outdoor TV and kitchen. There's nothing like swimming and watching football. Dave was trying to convert me to be a Rams fan while I was working on making him a Cowboy fan. One thing I really love is the sound of running water and by the touch of a button you had a refreshing waterfall flowing over the rocks and into the pool. We all fell in love with one another. Dave was happy to have us and Mandy was lovely. She has such a prophetic gift and develops the most amazing vision boards. Well, on that Saturday, we agreed that we would move in after church the next day.

We did that very thing. When my children saw the backyard they said, "Dad, it's the garden of Eden." I went to the airport for my early Monday morning flight with a heart full of gratitude and Joy. In a 24-hour period of time, the Lord took us from not knowing where we would be to the most opulent place we had ever been. Also, when I left the family there would be Mandy and Dave to look after them. They became family to us and still are. They are the most wonderful and caring people that I have ever met and just flat out fun. Can't tell you how many times we sat out back and Dave would say, "Hey, let's throw on some steaks!!" Well, you're talking my language! God was amazing to my family and once again super-naturally provided not just a place but went over and beyond giving us a place to stay that has become our West Coast Home. The kids loved "having" Molly as their dog. The kids could continue to go to Bethel. Many times Mandy and Sabrina would just fellowship and talk. We had some amazing prayer times together.

Now before this chapter ends, I will tell you that after I arrived back from Florida and was in the cottage for just a few hours, God gave me a vision. I was going out the door of the cottage and I was instantly in the Spirit. I saw the complete patio filled with people around the pool and sitting at the bar in the kitchen area. It looked like a hundred people or so. I knew instantly that God was going to have us do outdoor meetings at this place and minister to people. I closed the door then reopened it again and saw an empty patio. It was a vision. That was Oct 18th of 2018, I believe. He did it and that is another short story. When we were moving in, I told Mandy it will probably be just a couple of months that we are here. Mandy looked at me and smiled, "You gonna be here long time."

I said, "Really?"

She said again in her charming Puerto Rican accent, "You gonna be here Long Time."

She was right. We moved in October 14, 2018 and we abided with Christ and our new friends in that place until June 4, 2019. It was 233 days in case anyone is asking.

We still to this day laugh and cry tears of joy over our memories at Dave and Mandy's. We love their daughters and son-in-law Brandon They consider our kids grandkids. Faith is the victory that overcomes. I hope this chapter will inspire you to keep the faith when things LOOK desperate or when they LOOK outta control. The truth is they are not. Faith sees the end result while giving you the wisdom for the current moment. The first day that we were all in the cottage after my return from Florida, Mandy came to the front door and knocked. She said, "It's the widow of Zeraphath."

I opened the door. I said, "Yes, you are." We proceeded to tell her the story of reading 1 Kings 17 and knowing that God was sending a woman to sustain us. We laughed and cried all together. I told her, "You're not a widow but you are a woman who opened her home with her amazing husband to a family that was seeking to do the will of God."

Mandy said, "I need to show you guys something." She opened up her prayer book. She said, "I was praying last night and the Lord took me into this book. This is where I write things down that He shows me." She had tears in her eyes as she said, "Look right here. I don't remember writing this." She turned the book to us to read for ourselves. We looked at the few words and were stunned. We were in total wonder of the God who started this whole journey. The journey that turned into A FELLOWSHIP. The sentence said, "Take Tim and Sabrina and their children home to live with you."

We all stood in silence. I said, "That's before we got here." Before we had an idea that God would even send us to California, God put it by revelation into her heart to write those words.

She said, "Guys, I don't remember even writing this. I saw it last night written in red pen," which is how she designates a word from the Lord. This is a wonder and a mystery. But we knew that God had put us together. We knew that we were in the right place and that God had a plan. God will always have a plan. He will always have a woman in Zarephath for His men and women who are trusting Him. I end this chapter with this Word:

> *Trust in the Lord with all your heart. Lean not unto your own understanding. In all your ways acknowledge Him and He shall direct your path.*

MARK 11:24

Therefore I say unto you, What things soever ye desire, when ye pray, believe that ye receive them, and ye shall have them.

CHAPTER 16

Maximus Birthday Party

In the previous chapter, I told you how magnificent the property was that God provided for us. Soon after we moved to Mandy and Dave's place, they told us that they were going to be gone for a month from Thanksgiving to New Year. So basically we had our cottage and their house. Their house had a lovely kitchen so it made life a bit easier to make meals and such. We had Thanksgiving dinner at their table and just looked at each other with such gratitude to God. Dave told me to use his office as if it were my own. That was a great blessing. We were enjoying the place and doing a few meetings around the Riverside Area. We had met several wonderful people of God during this time. We were doing some TV appearances and ministering in church services. Sabrina would speak at some different events for ladies. It was an amazing and very blessed time.

We were experiencing the Blessing of Almighty God in wonderful ways. The Word says that Obedience is better than sacrifice in 1 Sam 15:22. When the Lord said to leave what we knew and everything that seemed familiar, we did it not because we are anything extraordinary. We did it because we loved the Lord. I always get chills when I hear Whitney Houston sing "I love the Lord." It goes on, "He heard my cry and pitied every groan. Long as I live, and troubles rise I hasten to His throne."

We just love the Lord. We obey Him and His Word because we **love** Him. In early April 2020, as I was washing dishes, the Lord spoke to me and said, "I'm going to prove myself to you. You will live better during this Crisis than you did before." The Crisis for those that will read this in the years to come was COVID-19. Everything was shutting down and we were headed to a place none of us had ever been. I will testify that it is true. The Lord has proven Himself over and over again. We have had "Ravens" show up. We have continued to minister to people over the phone, text or email even when traveling wasn't allowed or available. We had meetings canceled and for someone who travels for ministry that can be devastating. Yet our God has not only sustained us but has taken us to a rich abundance that is marvelous. Our two-year trip of faith required much of us. At times, it seemed too much. But our Faith was tested and has since grown to such a place that we simply receive what the Lord says without question. You know folks, God desires to be believed. If we believed God as much as we quickly believe the News Anchor, mighty things would happen in our lives.

I'm not scolding anyone. It's the toughest thing on the planet to believe in a God who is spirit. It is tough to take His Word as truth when everything around seems to be and say the opposite of what He has said. But that is the point. Believe God. Believe what He says and watch what He will do. Obedience is better when you obey because you love Him and desire His will. It's better because sacrifice can be the result of doing our own will and then trying to bribe God with a gift. Trust me, obey God.

Obeying God fills your soul with Joy. Many who I encounter in life and ministry look like they sit and suck on dill pickles. They have no life and no joy. It shows me that they have a life that isn't filled with obedience. For even in the most desperate times, our soul will be filled with this mysterious thing called Joy. Happiness, as the world defines it, is a result of everything just going your way; but Joy, my oh my, JOY is there when things *aren't* going our way. God Himself fills us. Strength is the result of Joy and Joy is the result of Obedience. We sing it, don't we? The joy of the Lord is my strength!!! Obedience is better because of Love.

Back to 2018: I recall Max coming to his mother and me with a desire to have his 14th birthday at Mandy's Place. Mandy and Dave were happy to say "yes." Max invited around 14 of his best friends from school and used all the different things to which we had access. So, we made plans to have everybody come over on a late Saturday morning and enjoy the property because it's always sunny in Sunny California, right??

The day of the birthday party I'm driving down the mountain to go to a men's breakfast. It was raining all the way there. I wasn't very happy about the circumstances. I was like, "God this Kid has been awesome. He deserves to have a great day for a birthday party. It's cold and rainy. What in the world are we gonna do?" Real Faith Man there, right? LOL. I was driving back up to the mountain and I couldn't see the mountain due to fog and rain. I was thinking, "This isn't good. What are we gonna do?"

I arrived back at the house and when I got through the gate and turned the corner, I saw something taped to the front door of the cottage and it was in Maximus's handwriting. It said the following!!!

Mark 11:22-24 And Jesus answering saith unto them, Have faith in God.

For verily I say unto you, That whosoever shall say unto this mountain, Be thou removed, and be thou cast into the sea; and shall not doubt in his heart, but shall believe that those things which he saith shall come to pass; he shall have whatsoever he saith.

Therefore I say unto you. What things soever you desire, when you pray believe that ye receive them, and you shall have them.

Right there I repented and said, "Lord. You are about to do something wonderful because even though my heart wasn't in faith, You had a soon to be 14 year old boy's faith up and going."

Mandy told me later in the day that when I was at the men's breakfast early that morning, she saw Max out walking in the rain with his hands up. She said, "Tim, it looked like he was talking to something." She said, "Then it hit me that he is speaking to the wind and the waves and saying, 'Peace Be Still. Glory to God.'"

As Max has grown up in our family, he has seen us move in the realm of the Spirit. He has witnessed wonderful provision, miraculous healing, and demons cast out. Plus he had heard the story of good ol' dad speaking to the winds and waves when he was a kid. I have told him the stories of my prayer meetings that I spoke of earlier in the book. He has always been a doer. He has seen and heard me preach that this life is available to everybody. God isn't a respecter of persons. It's open to whosoever will. We all may partake of the full faith of the son of God. Glory!!!

I walked into the cottage and there was Sabrina contemplating what back up plans we had for this birthday. There wasn't a "Hello, honey!" from being gone. She simply said, "We could go to a trampoline park or we could go to the pizza place and play games...!

I just kinda stood back still blown away by what I saw on the door. Max looks at his mom and says, "I don't wanna go anywhere. I just want to have my birthday party here. I don't bend to the weather, the weather bends to me." I was thinking again, "Where do you get this stuff?" Then it dawns on me, "OH Yeah." Looking outside it didn't look good. The palm tree was bending down in the wind and the wind was cold. We were in the mid 40's which isn't a southern Cal type of an afternoon. We decided to party and thank the Lord for His word. Max then says something that put me over the top and lit my faith fire. He said, "The Lord told me in the shower two weeks ago that my party would come off without any problems."

I said, "Wait? Let me get this straight. You have got a scripture on the front door **and** you have a *rhema* word from God?"

He said, "Yep."

I said, "I'm in." With that we looked outside and saw that the wind had subsided and now it was not raining either. Well, you gotta have a beginning and that was the beginning.

I said, "Let's go to the pool house and grab some towels. Let's start drying things off in faith. We were doing that very thing when I went to the basketball court to start sweeping the puddles off. I looked to the mountains in the distance and I saw blue sky about the size of a man's hand. LOL.

You remember the story in the Bible when they were believing for rain and the prophet sent his servant to look for a cloud. He said, "I see a cloud the size of a man's hand." Well, we reversed it. We saw blue sky the size of a man's hand. We kept on preparing. I was thanking God and praying in tongues. I tell you in just about 20 minutes you could look up and see half the property covered in blue sky and half cloudy. However, the blue continued to advance.

It was time for us to go pick up some of Max's friends. When we arrived back, it was beautiful and we had friends everywhere. We started the birthday and we peeled our jackets off because it was too warm to have them on. The kids were running around. We had the fire pit going. Kids were playing basketball and horse shoes. Eventually, all the kids would end up at the gazebo - the place where we would pray individually and pray as a family everyday. We soaked in Sabrina's vista that God gave her. The kids just talked, played, and enjoyed it all.

I was sitting at the bar with my feet up watching the NFL network. It was an old Super Bowl. I believe it was Pittsburg and Green Bay. Suddenly I had arms around me and it was Maximus, the birthday boy himself. He was ear to ear smiles. "Look what the Lord did for my birthday. We woke up to a monsoon and it's now a gorgeous day!"

Sabrina walked up with tears in her eyes and said, "Max, you have inspired me today, son, with your faith and believing the Word of God."

Max grabbed me and said, "This is where I got it."

Sabrina smiled and said, "That's for sure."

Why would God do that for a birthday party? Well, I believe that my kids have a special call on their lives. Part of this journey we took was to show those kids something so radical that no devil in Hell or some Liberal professor or University in the future could take out of them.

God is real. His Word works! We please Him when we are in faith. God will respond to faith for a birthday party to prove Himself. To prove that in the future you still call on Him as *El Shaddi* for more serious needs. Remember the story of my prayer meetings? These early experiences with the leading and provision of God is the only way we could have had the courage of faith to cross the ocean with dozens of people to go to Israel. Obedience builds faith and faith causes us to obey in the future for the big things. So to make it simple, God will provide a 13-year-old boy perfect weather for his birthday party so this young man will believe Him for the big things God has planned in the future.

Max had heard my story of how God told me to command the rain to stop when I was just 14 or 15 and it did. I said, "Son, happy birthday. You have reached another level in your walk with God when you start changing the weather."

Jesus said, "Peace be still," to the Wind and the Waves. In the gospel of John, He said we would do greater things. Why not start at a birthday party?

MATTHEW 18:12

How think ye? if a man have an hundred sheep, and one of them be gone astray, doth he not leave the ninety and nine, and goeth into the mountains, and seeketh that which is gone astray?

CHAPTER 17

Molly Takes Care of Gracie

This story always brings up emotion and gratitude in my and my wife's hearts. It started out simple enough. Dave Reed and his dog, Molly, have always enjoyed the mountain area around their home. Dave invited us on a walk that morning. As a family, we had gone on several walks with Dave. This time it was only Dave, Molly and my girls, Giselle and Gracie, and myself. We started out enjoying the weather and all the beauty of the rare flowers that had bloomed in California that year. We began to climb the mountain. Now we aren't talking about Everest or McKinley, but, it took some time and it was a great place to go up and survey the land and enjoy the area.

Now during our time with Dave and Mandy, Molly (as I have said) the kindest, most patient dog I had ever seen! The kind of dog you would prefer around a curious 6-year-old such as Gracie, who delighted in counting teeth. LOL. We would often find Molly and Gracie just talking and wandering around the property.

"Come on Molly," we would hear Gracie say many times during the day. Molly became Gracie's companion and keeper. Molly even began to come and sleep in the living room of the cottage at night. She literally became our family dog. We took her with us in the van to go and hike other places in the Riverside area. She was a beautiful dog. We always found it hilarious how she would come in from a walk and wade straight into the pool to cool off.

She was like a person. After Gracie would turn in for the night, Molly kinda became my friend. If I went up to pray in the Gazebo, she would come along. She was a li'l older now and didn't move as well as she used to, but she still made the effort to climb the hill in the back of the property to sprawl out on the floor while I would pray and talk with the Lord. Little did I know how valued this dog would become to me and my family.

We were reaching the top of the mountain. It was a place where Dave had been a hundred times before and we along with him a handful of times since our arrival. Gracie, whom I kept my eye on, and Giselle, who is a very independent and athletic girl, were in front of me. Dave and Molly pulled up the rear guard. We stood there for what I would say was a minute to a minute and a half just looking at how beautiful the area was.

Once we got to the top I seem to remember Gracie saying, "Oh, a rabbit!" but I didn't pay attention. I guess I have to take that indictment. I got to the top and relaxed for a minute. We gazed around and then began to make our way down when Giselle said, "Dad, where is Gracie?"

Now let me say. When you stand on top of this mountain, you can move a few steps and see easily down the sides of it. It would appear that there is no way someone could make their way down without you being able to see them for quite a distance.

Dave looked one way while Giselle and I looked another way. Gracie was gone! It was so impossible. I thought the rapture happened and Gracie was the only one ready! I mean she was GONE. One minute there and the next you couldn't find her down any side of the mountain. Then Dave yelled over and said, "Do you see Molly?"

I thought, "WOW! We lost my daughter and Molly?" Surely we could see Molly. That we be like seeing a large snowball run down the side of the mountain. Nothing! We couldn't see anything. I felt terror like I had never experienced. I can't imagine the White Throne of Judgment causing as much terror and concern as that moment had created in my life. Even now on this side of it—ever since this incident when I'm facing something challenging, I think of this story and then all of the sudden, it means nothing. No sweat, we are good, we can handle this.

Back to the moment, "My God, my daughter is gone! How?"

Dave went off to look in the direction that we had come from. Giselle went a little distance down the mountain and I went another. Giselle and I met up a few minutes later and nothing. Giselle was scared and so was I. Then we grabbed hands and prayed. We called out and said, "God, we are in Covenant with you. We cast out fear!" Then we began to declare the Word of the Lord over sister Gracie, my daughter. This went on for what seemed forever but it literally was about 50 minutes.

I was going down the other side of the mountain and it was so rocky and difficult I was thinking she slipped and she was hurt. But I knew that Molly wouldn't leave this kid no matter what. That was the only comfort we had that day.

Then I just sat down and pulled out the water bottle that I had and had a peace that truly passes all understanding come over me. I said with my mouth, "She has been found." I climbed back up to the top to start making my way down the other side. Dave had called his friend, Jim, and the police had been called and they would be getting ready to put a chopper in the air. This was happening quickly. Jim brought out his 4 wheeler to cover more ground. However, praise God, when I reached the top from the other side again, I could hear Dave yelling, "We have her! She is ok!"

I ran down the side of a mountain and did things that my then 48 year old body shouldn't have been able to do. I jumped river beds and ran through thorns. All to get to my girl that was lost Giselle was down there also. She was crying and I was crying too and Dave and Jim were all smiles.

It turned out that as we were looking around that Gracie had seen a small rabbit and immediately began to follow it with Molly by her side. Upon investigation, you could see how this path curled immediately below us into the mountain and created an optical illusion that made one think that you were looking straight down the mountain when really there was a path cut out that was kept from your view. Gracie had never been alone before, but she had Molly.

Gracie fell down a few times in the rugged land.
She began to pray and ask God to help her find us
or us find her. Then she told us, "After I fell the
last time and I prayed, the Lord spoke to me and
said, 'You just follow Molly. I have told her where
to take you.' " Glory to God, Oh what a Savior! He
speaks Dogish. LOL. Just follow Molly. I have told
her where to go.

Now on the side of the mountain that Gracie was
coming down, there was a lady sitting on her back
porch studying her Sunday school lesson. She
looked up to the mountain and saw a sight that
did not look right. "That little girl is too little to
be out by herself." She saw her fall several times.
And she saw that a Dog seemed to be leading her
down the mountain. The dog was waiting for her
during the times she would stop or trip or fall.
Such a Patient Dog, lovely Molly. Molly led Gracie
down the mountain into a dry river bed which
eventually led to the gate of this lady's yard. Now
this lady going down to meet Gracie could also
see Dave from her location and began to wave
her hands and call him over. That is where Dave
found her and brought her to the place where they
could call out to me and say we have her.

I tell you from that time on whenever Dave
grilled steaks, I always made sure that Molly, the
Wonder Dog, had a big chunk of steak. Anytime

we had it, she had a good part of mine. God told this Dog just where to lead my daughter so that she could be found. At the moment she was found was the same moment when on the other side of the mountain 'Peace like a River' poured over my soul and I knew that she was safe and had been found.

The police showed up just as we were getting back to Dave and Mandy's place. They asked Gracie a couple of questions and said we are glad she is safe.

Then Dave looked at me and said, "Uh, ya know, maybe you don't really need to tell this story to Sabrina?" Man, I was tempted, but I knew that my five-and-half-year-old daughter would tell the tale of her adventure with her Dog, Molly. So needless to say we were all very thrilled to have her back. Later as it got dark, I looked at every one and said, "What if? What if we hadn't found her?"

Maximus spoke up and said, "Well, we wouldn't be here talking about it. We would all be on the mountain still looking for her."

That is so true. This helped me understand the story of the shepherd leaving the 99 to go find the one. Some might say to relax since you have 99 healthy, wonderful sheep. They stayed with you. Why go after the ONE? Jesus was willing and still is willing to go after the one. I knew that what Max said was right. Didn't matter if we slept or ate, we would cover ground and we would discover every clue. We would find that which was lost. Jesus came to seek and save that which was lost. His Word says that He is not willing that even one should perish, but that all would come to repentance.

I'm thankful the day the voice of triumph in Heaven reached across the chasm of space and time and proclaimed, "We found him! We sought him and We found him." I was just 8 years old but my "being found" started a party in Heaven. We had a celebration for Gracie that night. We took her and bought her stuff. We got ice cream. We had a time of celebration. Celebrating "being found." That happens continuously in Heaven. "We found them! We found that which was lost."

The next day we went and took flowers to the lady who had seen Gracie coming down the mountain and had gotten Dave's attention. She said, "I was sitting there reading my Sunday school lesson for the next morning. I had just finished praying, 'Lord, use me in some small way to find those that are lost. Use Me.' " My God, my God, what an instant answer to prayer for that lady! We are grateful that she was seen by eyes that purposed to help and bring relief and safety. We were blessed to bless her. I can hear the old hymn of truth playing in my head and heart as I end this chapter.

Jesus loves me this I know

For the Bible tells me so...

Little ones to Him belong

They are weak, But He is Strong!!!

ACTS 5:16

There came also a multitude out of the cities round about unto Jerusalem, bringing sick folks, and them which were vexed with unclean spirits: and they were healed every one.

CHAPTER 18

The Meetings in Zeraphath

As I stated back in Chapter 15, I had a vision upon arriving and settling into the cottage on Mandy and Dave Reed's place. As a reminder, I was leaving for an errand when I opened the door and saw at least 100 people sitting around the pool area. People with camp chairs and blankets. They were all sitting and facing the same direction. I could tell it was a meeting that was getting ready to begin. I shut the door of the cottage and opened it again and they were gone. "Ok," I said to myself, "that was a vision. So, Lord, you are wanting us to do meetings here at Mandy's." I knew it would happen but just didn't know when.

I have found that the Lord will tell me something and 70% of the time it takes awhile for it to come to pass. The Lord is always wanting me to live in faith, to walk in the Spirit. I'm not reporting on what is happening around me but proclaiming what the Lord wants to bring to pass. So I told my wife and kids that we were going to do meetings here.

It would be fun outside and around the pool. It would be beautiful. But I saw this in Late October of 2018 and it didn't come to pass until April of 2019. I didn't tell anyone. I just remember Dave coming to me and saying outta nowhere, "Ya know, if you ever want to have a meeting or meetings up here you can. I have no problem with it." I simply looked at this as a confirmation of what the Lord showed me. I told Dave my vision and he said, "Great. Looks like we are on the same page."

Another thing about Dave is that he is so giving. When we came up to their place, we just had our Town and Country van. We didn't have a second vehicle. It would have been a blessing to have another. But, we didn't say anything. We just praised the Lord. We were a little further from the school by about 10 minutes and Giselle had started taking Ballet. We required another vehicle. I told Sabrina that the same God who had provided everything else would provide the transportation.

Well, here comes the Provision. Dave came over after we were there a couple weeks and said, "Hey, we have that Chevy Cruz sitting out there that our daughter owns. She is in Australia right now for a long time. Here are the keys. You just take it and use it as you need it." The Lord is good and His mercy endures forever. Another time that the Lord seems to just give us what we require with perfect timing.

Now on the onset of this Unimaginable Step of Faith, Sabrina and I and the family had no intention of coming to California let alone starting a Church. But, when the Lord showed me to do meetings at Mandy's and just let those around the area know, it got out that we were having seed meetings to start a church. Well, we tried our best to tell people that was not the case. The Lord wasn't calling us to start a church at that time. We simply were obeying the Lord.

One thing about Obeying the Lord, you can't wait until the time is perfect or move when everybody is finally going to be happy with you. As long as the Lord has given a direct command to run, you run.

There were changes going on in some local congregations and some thought our meetings were to take advantage of the people who were "bleeding" out from local churches. There was blood in the water. Now let me say, we had people coming to us that had the money, influence and savvy to help us start a church and it was offered to us. We could have had our own church without any of the normal stresses that many go through to start a church. Plus we could have easily started with probably 150 people. Many told me that we should. However, I do nothing without the leading of the Holy Spirit. Plus, Sabrina and I are not Sharks. We could see the blood in the water from other ministries that were in transition. We are called to heal and help, to restore and bring life.

You can only tell people once or twice that you're not doing something but people believe what they want to believe. My job is to obey God. We set a date and in early April we had a meeting at Dave and Mandy's House. Like I mentioned in Chapter 15, their place was a distance out of town and by the time you felt good and lost, there's their neighborhood. LOL. Evan and Shawnna Perez brought a sound system with speakers and a microphone so I was able to hook-up my iPad to sing and play tracks. I wondered who would come and what would go on. As the time came near, we had absolutely amazing weather. It was cool but not cold. I walked out of the cottage and our stage was the fire pit. It raised up by 5 inches or so and made for a great pulpit. People came with camp chairs and others went over into the grass and put blankets out. We had kids running around the property.

Then a friend who I hadn't seen in years came to the meeting with his family and his guitar and led worship for us. We had 87 people at that meeting. We worshipped for a while and then my daughters and Tatum Perez did a lovely dance and then Sabrina got up and shared for a bit.

Now it was my turn and, man, you could cut the anointing with a knife. The power of God was evident. The natural energy of being outside was there also. You could imagine that this was similar to a setting like when Jesus taught;. outside, the adults sitting and the children off in the grass playing chase. It wasn't a distraction; it was a beautiful thing. I spoke and preached for a while and the Lord was using us.

In the very beginning when people were coming in, a couple came in and sat right on the front. I had never seen these people before. Later on, the husband, Brad, told me that they came with great expectation. I didn't know it, but their little girl was best friends with our little girl Gracie and went to Bethel also. They heard about the meeting and just felt drawn by the Holy Spirit. Well, Brad and his lovely wife, Heather, were right on the front row. Brad didn't really know much about the move of the Holy Spirit. He had seen his sister's church on TV and people falling under the power of God. He said with a healthy dose of skepticism, "That can't be real and I want nothing to do with it."

Well, the Lord gave Brad and Heather a front row seat and the very first thing I did was call a lady up outta the crowd and the word of prophecy came for her and we laid hands upon her and she felt the power of God so much that she went out. Now the pool patio was concrete and as she went down we had people to help. But the funny part is that her head came to rest on Brad's tennis shoe. LOL. God has a great sense of humor, huh? He told me later when her head hit his shoe, he knew beyond a shadow of a doubt that this was real.

Later in the meeting, we asked for people who needed a touch of healing in their body to come forward and we would pray. The line filled with people needing a touch from God. We started to lay hands on people and the power of God was present to heal. I would ask people what the problem was and they would say, "I can't really lift my right shoulder beyond this point." Then they would demonstrate their seeming disability and raise their arm completely up and they would dance and shout. People were in a line to be healed and looked shocked when it happened. God must laugh. We prayed for knees and every other type of thing that night. We had a lady who was deaf in one ear receive her hearing. Like I said in Chapter 12, we didn't ask God to heal anybody. We already knew that the stripes were taken 2,000 years ago. Jesus came to seek and save that which was lost. He said, "If you have seen me, you have seen the Father." Is it the Father's desire to heal? Look at the life of Jesus. If you have seen Jesus, then you have seen the Father. We know that God so loved the world that He gave His only begotten Son, why? To seek and save!! There is nothing to debate here. He is the Healer; He is the Provider. So we spoke to the body parts directly and reminded them of the stripes and that Christ had already died to bring them Healing. People were having miracles happen that night.

Evan Perez, who works in the medical field as an Anesthesiologist, was a catcher that night. That means he helped those who couldn't help themselves. He lowered them to the concrete. LOL.

He told me later, "You know, Tim, that every person that came forward to be healed was healed. 100% of those prayed for were healed." We had one gentleman there that was going in for surgery on his knee the next day. During prayer, his pain left immediately and he did not require the surgery. Now after this happened and people were prayed for, I looked down at the couple, Brad and Heather. They were crying and had the glory of God all over them. At that time, they had only been saved for six months. They were precious though they didn't look like church goers. Brad looked like a bouncer, but he was a successful business owner. I pulled both of them up and laid hands upon them and began to pray over them. Then the Lord gave me very detailed prophetic words over them. He had tears upon tears. His hands were raised and he was praising God. He came into the meeting not believing that this type of thing was real.

Now remember they were only saved six months prior. He looked at me and said, "Damn, man, how did you know all that stuff?" I tell you, we all laughed. If you can believe it, some folks get uncomfortable when I tell that story. But that was who he was and Jesus was in his heart and soul. I told them that the Lord knows everything about them and loves them. That He had wonderful plans for them to bless them and use them in this wonderful Kingdom; a kingdom with a King who knows your name and loves you.

What a night! People were blessed and God was so faithful. We had another meeting in May and then a final one before we departed Riverside. That meeting was on June 4, 2019.

The first was the largest, but we had people come out every time under the blue sky - seeking

Jesus. I knew when He told me to do it that we would have three meetings. We did.

I always smile when thinking about these meetings. I remember early in the first meeting, I looked over at Dave and Mandy. Mandy had told Dave, "You don't have to stay, honey. Go across the street and be with Jim."

Dave said, "No I wanna stay."

I looked over and there was Dave with tears in his eyes when he was watching our daughters and Tatum dance in the first part of the service. It is a wonder to see God deal with the hearts of men. I recently had the Lord speak to me while washing dishes. (Men, give your wife a break now and then and wash the dishes; the Lord will speak to you.) He said, "I'm going to prove myself to you in this situation." It struck me, "Lord, how meek and mild you are and all powerful to look at me, one man, on this planet dealing with a situation. You then say, 'I'm going to prove myself to you.'"

He is wonderful and beyond description. My mentor and friend, Dr. Lord Helm, used to say, "Walking with Jesus is Thrills, Romance and Adventure!" It is…it really, really is.

ROMANS 5:2

By whom also we have access by faith into this grace wherein we stand, and rejoice in hope of the glory of God.

CHAPTER 19

Before the Midnight Cry

I am excited to share this next story. This has been a joy to write and I have found myself overcome with Joy as I have reviewed the blessing and provision of the Lord during our Journey. When we left our home in Aiken, SC, my wife asked, "How long do you think we will be out?" Truthfully I didn't know, but I couldn't imagine being out for more than 90 days. I mean where would we go? I wasn't out to prove anything. I wasn't trying to make a name for myself. We, as a family, were simply trying to obey God.

I know what it feels now to be Abram, because he left everything he knew and followed God. During his journey, he became a different man; so much so that God changed his name to Abraham, father of many nations. May I say that Abraham was called "Father of many" when he hadn't even fathered one? God is like that ya know. He will put us in situations that are completely impossible. Yet when we trust Him and give Him the glory during these times, He will bring us through. He will make a way. But we must resolve within to simply follow. There is no sunrise without night, no water without rain clouds, and no resurrection without death. We must be willing to be put in the storm for Christ to walk up and say, "Be not afraid. It is I."

I sometimes wonder about the story of Lazarus. You *know* that Jesus liked to stay in Bethany where "LaZ" and his sisters lived. I have wondered and imagined if Jesus let him in on what was gonna happen. Indulge my hypothetical conversation.

"Listen, Lazarus, you are gonna die. I'm not showing up while you're still alive. Your sisters are gonna get upset. But that is the point I gotta bring them to the place where they know me as the resurrection and the life. Don't say anything about this, ok, Lazarus?"

Lazarus responds, "OK, Lord, whatever it takes. I am your servant and friend."

Of course, I'm not saying that is what happened. As I said, it is my imagination. I find it funny that the Scripture never talks to Lazarus or gets his side of the story. Yet he is the central figure in one of the most brilliant stories of the Bible. He was simply willing. Can you imagine if I'm correct in my wondering here? The sisters had sent for Jesus. They are trying to take care of Lazarus, but the Savior doesn't come and Lazarus knows all along that he is gonna die. *Somebody gotta be dead for four days and have them dreams stink to high heaven.* (That's my Southern-style paraphrase of John 11:39!) It's a part of the plan.

The Bible says that he who seeks to save his life shall lose it. But he that loses his life shall find it. Taking up the Cross of Christ isn't about going to and fro on the earth and seeking death or persecution. The Cross of Christ started in Gethsemane when He said, "Nevertheless, not my will, but thine, be done." We ought to be doing the Will of God whether or not it's convenient. We may wish to go another direction especially when things seem obvious to us, but the Spirit of God may say, "Not yet." He may check our hearts and we examine it for resistance. When God says, "Hold," don't go! Don't move... Wait.

Seeking your life and working things out according to how things look to you is saving *your* life. Doing what the Spirit leads when it is in total opposition to your flesh is *finding* your life.

The challenge to surrender the self to the Savior is a very simple Kingdom principle but it's not easy by any stretch of the imagination. Faith is the evidence of things not seen. What you require is in the Unseen. It's learning that there is a place called the Unseen. Here is what I believe. I'm not writing this book to push doctrine. I love to read the kinda book I'm writing. I love stories of the faithfulness of God. Stories of Faith. Believing God in spite of the circumstances. I believe that when you are born that everything that you could possibly require has been set aside for you in your heavenly account. But, this account is not only filled with money. It is filled with people, connections, favor! It's there to help fulfill whatever the call of God is on your life. It is set aside. That is really why I ask God for nothing but thank Him for everything.

Going back to Lazarus' story, you don't see Jesus begging the Father for anything. Jesus said, "Father, I thank You that You hear me." I have found this to be the best way to go about life. My friend Rodney Howard-Browne would say during services and while ministering to people, "Thank you, Lord Jesus." Continually saying, "Thank you, Lord Jesus." I adapted that into my life years ago and that is how I walk around and you can sneak up to any of my children's rooms and hear them going about whatever but they are saying, "Thank you, Lord Jesus."

Thanksgiving. If you wanna ask, that's fine. But for me and for what has worked, it has been Thanksgiving. Why? I have a revelation of something. It's already mine. It's already been set aside. A few months ago my wife and I had a $2,500 need. Now I looked at the date. It was early October of 2019. I have what I call a Purchase Order or as many would call it a PO. Many companies will not order anything without getting authorization from their purchasing agent. That agent gives them a purchase order and gives them the ability to access what they need.

Well, I have a purchase order that I have written out. Yes, it is a literal piece of paper. I basically put in the order to my heavenly account and I use all the scriptures of provision. My God shall supply all of my need according to His Riches in Glory by Christ Jesus. Also I go to Mark 11:22-25 and speak to the mountain and don't allow doubt to cloud my heart. I put the amount of money that I need and then we sign it. It is a place to put my faith. It's place of engagement to put into operation what the Lord told us to do.

Now, back to my October 2019 PO: we did that and about 17 days later we received a check in the mail for $2,500.00. I got that file out and looked at the Purchase Order and told the Lord, "I consider this transaction finished." Then I praised and thanked Him. For what it's worth, you don't have to do what I do, but do get a physical point of connection. It's like a prayer cloth or the use of oil for healing.

Now I believe that if I have a need in October of 2019 that God set aside what I needed in my heavenly account 49 years earlier when I was born. However, it probably was set aside at the beginning of time. That's how awesome God is. He knows our every need. So, when I go to Him in Faith I already know that He knows my need before I could even ask and He is always ready to provide. So I tell Him what I need and thank Him for it. Then I just continue to praise Him until what I need shows up. I have seen it with money, connection, homes, cars, vans, and manifold examples of favor. He always works things out after the counsel of His own will. It's in His Word. We must realize that He is our Father. He has everything that we need and more.

While traveling on this faith journey, we experience transformation. What used to freak us out in the past won't phase us in the future because our faith muscle gets bigger. God changes us. We begin to realize that if we feel like we're climbing a mountain to sacrifice Isaac, God summons a Ram to make his way up the other side of the mountain to be our provision.

During our Florida years, we lived in a great place west of Orlando called Celebration. We had passes to Disney World. It was a wonderful time in my family's life. My kids were really small and we had a ball. We would eat dinner and then go over to Disney. We could see the Epcot fireworks from our house. It was lots of fun and great family time. Occasionally, we would go over after dinner and find a spot to watch the parade. I don't really enjoy parades, but the kids and Sabrina love them. However, the Lord taught me a few things through the parades. I usually enjoy the end of the parade with Snow White and then Cinderella and Mickey. When I was on the ground, I could only see what was coming down the pike at that time. But if I were in a helicopter, then I could see the end from the beginning. I have to believe that God knows what is coming and He sees all. As a matter of fact, He is the Author and Finisher.

When it comes to receiving things that are yours from the Unseen, you really have to go to the Word. Romans 5:2 teaches "By whom also we have access by faith into this grace wherein we stand, and rejoice in hope of the glory of God." Notice the word access into this grace. Grace is the ability of God. You have probably heard someone say, "She is just graced to do this or that." Well, it's God's favor, it's God's ability. This place of grace is our storehouse of provision to be able to do what God has for us to do. We know that Hebrews 11:6 says without faith it is impossible to please God. So we have access into this grace (the Unseen place where all our things are stored and released for completion of our mission). By what? Faith. Faith is the hand that reaches into the realm of grace and draws out what is required for that moment. This is very easy to understand. Once you get it, you got it.

Know that God isn't keeping anything **from** you. He is keeping it **for** you. There is a time of fellowship and worship. It helps to see God do the littlest things that build faith. As our faith grows, we can put more of a demand on it. I taught my children this and it is amazing the things that they can believe into their lives now. They enjoy Dad and Mom getting them things. However, they know that God can and will supply for them. There is no waiting till you're 21 to drink in this Kingdom. All that He has is available and He loves it when we come after it no matter how old we are.

I remember getting ready to make a trip back to Tennessee while we were living in the cottage. I was flying back to minister in two great churches led by friends of mine. The Lord spoke to me and said, "I want you to believe me for $6,000 from this trip." Well, OK that would be awesome. I knew God was building my faith and taking us further. He had done this with me only one other time that I could remember. Also, like God, He likes to tell me to believe for results that have nothing to do with the reality that is in front of me. He invited me to get into agreement with Him and reply, "Ok," then Praise Him for the result. I said, "Lord, these churches will do their best to bless me, but I don't think it's reality to get $6,000 from these meetings." But, because He said it, I believed it.

I told my wife and the kids because I prefer for them to know these things. It's a faith exercise for us as a family to be able to be excited when things come through. Well, I was gonna be gone for about 7 days. The first meetings were amazing and people stepped up to bless us. Then I got a call from Sabrina that a person had sent a check for $1000 and then another sent a check for $1,000 outta nowhere. The second set of meetings were awesome. Again the people just blessed us in such a wonderful way. However, I was amazed when I put all the giving together from the services and then the unexpected giving that came in through the mail. When I landed in Riverside, the total was $5,500. I was like, "Well that is wonderful and it will take care of some needs that the ministry has for now, so praise God." But, I knew God said to believe Him for $6,000. You need to understand something to believe correctly. God isn't a counterfeiter. He doesn't print money. He follows His Word. Matthew 6:38 - "Pressed down, shaken together and running over shall men give into your bosom." God uses people. There are eight billion people on this planet. A wonderful man of God in Deming, New Mexico, helped me to see this. His name is Jeff Sutton and he pastors Living Word in Deming. If God uses people, then there are eight billion different avenues of possible blessing for you. God can get it to you no problem.

Well, back to the story. I landed about 4 p.m. and we were all glad to be back together again. I was thankful and I was still believing God for the full $6,000. But at 9 p.m., I was "turning into a pumpkin" and headed for bed. I said, "Lord, I know you said $6,000, but I'm thankful for this $5,500 that came in over the last seven days. At 11:45 p.m., fifteen minutes before midnight, Sabrina woke me up in the most funny way. She had five crisp $100 bills in her hand and she was brushing them up against my nose. LOL!!! She then said, "This makes $6,000."

I said, "What in the world? I have been asleep. Tell Me. Tell Me!"

Sabrina said that Mandy came over and had gotten home at 11:30 p.m. that night with a box that was given to her by a woman at the meeting who wished to remain anonymous. The box was full of canned goods and a razor set for me, toilet paper, and just great stuff. But there was a paper envelope in the box also. It was so late and Mandy said, "I am sure they are asleep. I will give it to them tomorrow." God shook Mandy in her Spirit and said, "You go back and knock on the door NOW, I WANT THEM TO HAVE IT NOW!!!" Sabrina was awake and Mandy gave her the box. After they chatted briefly, Sabrina opened the envelope...and there was $500. It completed the $6,000 God had told us we would receive.

Now remember, I had just flown in a few hours earlier so it was still the last day of my trip. My wife woke me up and God provided the last bit - the last $500 arrived fifteen minutes before midnight. Now you know why I titled this chapter "Before the Midnight Cry!" Oh, Glory to God! There is nothing too hard for Him!

Not only can God get the things to you that you require, He can get you anywhere He requires you to be. On one of our visits to San Francisco, I remember the Lord saying to me, "Go to City Hall." I had just finished a tour at the Disney Family Museum and when the Lord gave me that command I had a feeling that I would meet the Mayor of San Francisco.

When I got to City Hall, there was a tour just about to begin so I joined the tour. As we walked through City Hall, the tour guide announced that San Francisco had a new female mayor named London Breed. "I've worked here for 6 months and I haven't seen her," the security guard had said, "they must bring her up the back way or something." I chuckled. I thought, "I better go check her office." So, I stopped in her office, but her assistant said that she wasn't there.

There happened to be a press conference in one of the rooms so I left the tour to go to check it out. It turned out that the Mayor London Breed was congratulating a group of entrepreneurs from Malaysia. I stood on the sidelines as she was wrapping up. The next moment, Mayor Breed was walking off the stage and we met face to face. I said, "Hi, can I get a picture with you?"

She said, "Sure!" I handed my phone to one of her assistants who was apparently bewildered by the function of a smartphone. While we waited for the picture, I mentioned that my family and I were praying for her. I got to give her a word concerning the City of Francisco. After two minutes the picture was taken and I was on my way.

On my way out the door, I saw the same security guard and showed her the picture of Mayor Breed and myself. She freaked out, "How did you do that?

"Favor, baby, favor," then I walked out into the cold pouring rain.

God said, "I can get you to anyone, anywhere, saying the right words at the right time if you will just follow and trust Me." So He can get funds to ya. He can get you to a City Official. He can get you to the companion, job, college, career, or church that is meant for you, no matter what.

> "He is faithful that called you, who will also DO IT!!" I Thessalonians 5:24

II TIMOTHY 1:7

For God hath not given us the spirit of fear; but of power, and of love, and of a sound mind.

CHAPTER 20

Release Fear, Embrace Faith

Against all hope, Abraham hoped and believed and thereby became the father of many nations. It would seem that in order to have the ability to multiply and become, we must have the ability to hope when there seems to be nothing to justify that hope.

All Abraham had was a Word from God. And, so BECAME—this verb means transformation! A metamorphosis transpired in this biblical account. That is one of the many purposes of this wonderful story. That we can change; we can become. That wonderful Christ in us - the Hope of Glory. The Hope? The ability to emerge into what God intended. We may start at one place, limited and inferior, but within us is Christ. The one by which the Universe became what it is. The Word says all things were created by Him and through Him. We see that Abram wasn't a perfect man. He was a man that battled with fear. He also lied because of that fear. Yet, God still worked through him so that all of the families of the earth are blessed because through obedience Abram became Abraham.

In this book I have shared many triumphant stories. Facts tell, stories sell. Am I trying to sell you something? Yes! Yes I am. I am trying to sell you on the fact that God has a wonderful plan for your life. You were born with purpose. You are not a mistake. God doesn't daily rub His head and say, "HMMMM, what am I gonna do with this one?"

Your destiny does not pivot on your abilities or your circumstances - no matter how wonderful or hard your circumstances may be. Abraham had something going for him. He simply believed God. He didn't look at the deadness of Sarah's womb, nor that his body was old and without ability. God said!

Isn't this really the question? The serpent offered this in the garden in the beginning. "Hath God Said?" He knew that if he could get man to question what God had said, then he could stop man in his tracks. The Bible says that God is pleased with faith. God is pleased when we simply take Him at His word. Regardless, love this word without regard to the situation that you find yourself in today. God is able. God is willing. God is Faithful; the great I AM!!

That is basically what I have wanted to get across to you and to all who read this book. BELIEVE GOD! If He said It in His Word then it's a fact and you can believe it. Speak it and live in that promise. You may never be called to absolutely leave everything the way we did. That isn't the point. We did what God told us to do. We can look at many people that have been helped and blessed. Folks who were launched into ministry and who are now pursuing their call because we simply obeyed God.

The assignment ended in June of 2019. We felt we were to return to Aiken, SC, and set up shop again and wait on God to see what was next. My wife has always had a desire to live on a farm. Well, today we live on 30 acres with a lake that has ducks and a pony named Tiny Dancer. The beautiful farm house is historic and feels like we live in the Gone with the Wind movie minus the Civil War.

Our children have come back to accomplish many things. Max became MVP of his middle school in Basketball and a Scholar Athlete. Giselle came back to join the Colton Ballet as the second girl ever in the 50 year history to be asked to join as a company girl at the age of 11. God answered the desire of her heart; she was given the leading role of Clara in the Nutcracker for Christmas. Our youngest has been in the choir at our church and has been singing all over the area. Our family is blessed. We are back where we started, but the blessing of the Lord has overtaken us here. It's not the same Aiken that we left. We don't know if we will always live here. But, it's where we are for now and God is blessing us. We do see that our stepping out in the way that we did lifted our faith to a different level.

You may never be called to do what we did. Our desire is for you to launch out and do what He is telling you to do. Allow me to urge you to obey God and begin the preparation. Maybe you require some education to do what God has called you to do. Are you stepping out by faith to do it? Or are you sitting back with excuses why you can't accomplish His will for you in this life?

When my girls wanted the pony that we currently have now at our farm, we began to look and you would think it would be easy to find a horse in Aiken, SC!! There are more polo fields here than any other place in America. You might as well call this place **ROHAN**! (*Lord of the Rings* fans, can I get a witness?) We are Horse People.

We couldn't find a pony. But we looked around on our property and we have stables. So, if God gave us stables, He must have a pony for us. So we quit looking and decided to put our faith out there to go to work. My girls went and let faith take action. They cleaned up the stable and got it ready for a pony. The girls did what they could. We didn't expect God to send the angels to earth to clean up the place. They put their faith in action. I will ask you now. Is your faith active? Are you doing what you can now towards what you are believing God for or for what He has put in your heart?

Then I took the girls out to the stables and we poured a small dot of oil on the ground. We prayed and released our faith. Faith is a servant. We simply released it and said, "Go get our pony."

Well, about two and a half weeks later our friend who runs a polo horse farm behind our property for a well known polo player called my wife and said, "Listen, I was in Virginia this past weekend picking up some horses from a farm." The family asked if we would take their pony "Tiny Dancer" down to the farm to enjoy the weather and just chill a bit. The pony had been with them for 20 years and their children had ridden the pony but were all grown now. She told the family about us. The family said, "Yes, if they will love her and care for her, they can keep her on their property." Beth and her staff put things together, fixed fences, gave us a saddle and other necessities and in the blink of an eye that spot of oil sprouted a beautiful pony for free! Notice the name "Tiny Dancer?" My girls are both dancers. However, they didn't name the pony. The pony was named "Tiny Dancer" 20 years before. Seven years before my oldest girl, Giselle, was born, this pony was named for her and her sister.

That, my friend, is a God that knows no limits, that has love that I cannot understand nor conceive of. We couldn't find a pony through earthly sources because God wanted to provide through heavenly sources. (The tears are just running down my face as I write this.) Just a little while after returning to Aiken, SC, the Lord spoke to me and said, "I'm going to show my love for your children." Well, my God has fulfilled His word. As Abram became Abraham, I must say that each of my family members became and grew to be a greater version of themselves. Our children have continued to believe God and see continuous provision in their lives. Their love for Jesus is inspiring to their mother and me. Speaking of their Mother, I, as her husband, am amazed that she was willing to take this journey, giving up what most women would not. However, to see how God speaks to her and moves in her life is a thing of true beauty. Proverbs 31 come to life is a picture of Sabrina Gidley.

As I write these final words of this book, I must say it has been amazing to rehearse these experiences and the life of my family with you, the reader. I can't imagine where this book will go or how many libraries it will find its way into, however, if we inspire you to reject fear and embrace FAITH, we have done our job. The reason we left our home was to show that the same God that told Abram to leave his home and become a Father of many nations is truly what His Word says He is. He is the same yesterday, today, and forever. If we inspire you to go take the class, preach the sermon, start the online video channel for Christ, bake a cake, or start that Bible study. If God is calling you to do something, fear will always rise and yet faith is always available. It's already in you. You have the same faith as Peter or Paul. It's the faith of the Son of God.

He will use your obedience to inspire others, who will in turn inspire others. Then in eternity to come, you will see what your obedience, no matter how small it looked to you, did, and what it accomplished for His glory. Finally, you will say with your actions of faith and obedience, "I am not ashamed of the Gospel." He's been faithful and taken us truly beyond what we can see and well beyond our Unimaginable Step of Faith.

The Perez Family Testimony

During a Sunday service at Bethel, which was my church of 28-years in Riverside California, Tim and his family shared their tremendous testimony of leaving South Carolina in order to fulfill God's call on their lives. That very Sunday afternoon, driving home, the Lord asked me a question. "Evan—would you leave behind everything for Me?" Immediately I replied, "everything!?" I could sense in my Spirit that God was not kidding. So, I answered, "Well Lord—for You, I would have to be obedient. Especially if You asked me to." In my soul, I made that decision right then and there. It was a huge moment. All the while Shawnna and our two kids, Tatum and Hunter, were sitting in the car, completely oblivious of the "big decision" that I had just made. At that very moment, God said, "Tell your family what I asked you and give them your answer!" Straightening up in my seat and clearing my throat, I confidently said, "Just to let everyone know—if God ever asks us to leave everything, our home, relatives, friends, my job, your school, this country—we would!" The shock, awe, and frustration that I believed would erupt out of my loved ones, never followed. My son of 3-years, who had just started preschool and had recently made a handful of new friends, joyfully asked, "When are we leaving!?" From there, the journey began.

A few weeks had gone by and my family and I were attending a young girl's birthday party. This young girl happened to be a classmate of my daughter and was also a friend of Giselle. As God would have it, Giselle and Sabrina were also at the birthday party that day. Immediately the divine connection and love began to grow. We spent the entire party sharing with each other about God's grace and love, especially in our families' lives. God also gave me a prophetic word for Tim and Sabrina, that the Lord had me share with Sabrina. Sabrina kept telling us, "You all have to meet Tim! I have never heard anyone else speak like my husband!" About a week later Tim contacted our family and we met at the McMeans' house, where Tim and his family were temporarily staying. We shared many amazing testimonies and had the privilege of prophesying over each other's family members. From that point, the bond and friendship grew

even stronger. When the time had come for Tim
and his family to move to another residence,
Shawnna and I had a strong desire to sow into their
ministry, but in more ways than just financially.
We truly desired to have a place large enough for
them to stay while they were living in California,
though our home was far too small for the nine of
us to abide. In January 2018, the Lord provided an
opportunity for us to help Tim and Sabrina. We
were so honored when they asked us to care for
their children for 10-days while they traveled to
Israel to minister. We had such a blessed time with
Max, Giselle, and Gracie-belle.

Many years before Shawnna and I had children,
the Lord spoke to us about homeschooling
our children. We had unknowingly allowed
fear to detour that decision from coming to
fruition. One afternoon, Shawnna and Sabrina
were fellowshipping and something Sabrina
said reignited that instruction from God to
homeschool our children. Tatum, our 8-year
old daughter at that time was in third grade.
Hunter, our 4-year old son was still in preschool.
Tatum had been in private school for five years
now and had established many friendships. In
conversation, she had voiced her opinion of not
wanting to be homeschooled, for concern of
losing friends. My wife and I went to the Lord
in prayer, petitioning that He would place the

desire to be homeschooled in her heart. Our family was leaving to go on our second mission trip, this time to Honduras. Before leaving, Tim gave us a word that "the Lord is going to show us specifics about our ministry and give us clarity and direction." The Lord indeed, showed us our next steps. It was now Thanksgiving break and music to my ears. Tatum, out of nowhere, asked me if she could be homeschooled from now on. She begged to not go back after Thanksgiving break. After Christmas break, we began our homeschooling journey thanks to Sabrina being obedient and sensitive to share what the Holy Spirit had placed on her heart. In December of 2018, my Pastor of 28-years from the pulpit announced his retirement. As I walked out of the sanctuary, immediately after hearing the news, the Lord spoke to me and said, "this is your last day here." In utter amazement, I said, "okay Lord, where are we supposed to go?" Week by week the Lord had us "on assignment/in training" guiding us to attend certain churches for a very specific duration. Now, of course, we look back and know this was training to be more in-tune and obedient to God's direction on our lives. Now in February 2019, the Lord spoke, telling me to cut down to part-time status at work. Yet, I was still to sow financially off of my full-time pay. At the time this did not make a lot of sense. Ever since I was a young boy the Lord showed me that I was to financially sow millions into the ministry. I was under the impression that I needed a full-time job to fulfill this vision/desire. He has been so faithful in every area!

During New Year's 2019, our family along with the Gidley family had a New Year's Eve time of prayer and vision board writing. The Lord showed my wife that we were to go on three mission trips in 2019. At the time, we were approaching August, and still no mission trip on the books. We went before the Lord and reminded ourselves of His promises over our family. Not more than a week later, we had a divine connection with a couple who had been praying and seeking for someone to help them go out and serve the people of Tijuana, Mexico. Upon the completion of 2019, our family completed four mission trips.

At the end of May, the Lord woke me up in the middle of the night and said, "register for your doctorate program in anesthesia." Mind you, I wanted to further God's kingdom and not my anesthesia career. With only a week's notice, the deadline to register was fast approaching. God showed me exactly what school I was to attend and I supernaturally was accepted into the program. Tim gave me a word that the Lord was going to use my doctorate to get me into places for kingdom purposes. By August I had started school.

Today, God has Shawnna and I hosting a full-time discipleship Bible study in our home every Saturday. We host "watch parties" or online church services, every Sunday morning and Wednesday evening. We have started an online discipleship Bible study with people all over the world. Once again, last year during an intimate family Bible study with the Gidley family, Tim prophesied that Shawnna and I would be online sharing God's Word. Here we are fulfilling God's word, hallelujah! When God asked me if I would leave everything for Him, it has not looked the way I imagined it would look. Yet, it has been so amazing and better! God is so kind and gentle in His leading. We truly serve such a kind and faithful Father. As well, we are eternally grateful and tied together in love with Tim and his beautiful family. Their fervent love and obedience to God's calling on their lives, is inspiring to say the least. My family's faith has been stirred-up to a greater degree than ever before thanks to Tim, Sabrina, Max, Giselle, and little Gracie-belle. God bless you—brother!

Tim Gidley

Tim celebrates 23 years in full-time ministry and music. Having recorded 8 solo projects, Tim has shared the Gospel in 15 countries of the world, most beloved being Israel where he has led several pilgrimages over the last 5 years. Tim's ministry has been received via many conferences and churches as a keynote speaker and soloist. In addition, Tim has also sung for political events such as the Republican National Convention.

Tim has a passion for helping the local church reach their full potential in the winning of souls and changing the way people think. Failure in every area of life can be traced to improper thought patterns. That is a primary reason for making the leap into becoming an author. Leaders are readers.

Through Crown Voice Ministries, Tim and his wife, Sabrina, want to provide content that helps launch the believer into a life of Faith and Christ-centered strategy. Tim and Sabrina have been married for 21 years and live on a farm with their 3 children, many animals, and a hamster named Peanut Butter.

Made in the USA
Columbia, SC
14 September 2021

44732294R00117